First-Time
Machine Appliqué

BY JANET PITTMAN

Landauer Publishing, LLC

First-Time
Machine Appliqué
BY JANET PITTMAN

Copyright © 2013 by Landauer Publishing, LLC

This book was designed, produced, and published by Landauer Publishing, LLC
3100 101st Street, Urbandale, IA 50322
515-287-2144 / 800-557-2144; www.landauerpub.com

President/Publisher: Jeramy Lanigan Landauer
Vice President of Sales & Administration: Kitty Jacobson
Editor: Jeri Simon
Art Director: Laurel Albright
Photography: Sue Voegtlin

Library of Congress Control Number: 2013933179

ISBN 13: 978-1-935726-34-0

This book is printed on acid-free paper.

Printed in United States

10 9 8 7 6 5 4 3 2 1

Table of Contents

Welcome to my world of machine appliqué.

Follow these nine lessons—from supplies, fabric, and thread through preparation and stitching— for a step-by-step look at great techniques to make appliqué quick and easy.

I have been designing machine appliqué since 1995, the same year I bought a new sewing machine with 34 programmed stitches. The stitches reminded me of the hand embroidery my grandmother taught me when I was young. I knew I wanted to use those stitches and although I admired hand appliqué, I worked full time and wanted to get my appliqué images quickly onto fabric. As I experimented I saw the potential for using the programmed stitches to add my grandmother's touch to quick appliqué projects.

There are two major techniques for machine appliqué preparation. One uses paper-backed fusible web to stabilize the edge and the other requires making a turned-under edge. The biggest difference between the two techniques is the kind of corners and points you can make. In the photo, the heart on the left, prepared with fusible web, is very pointed. You can prepare more sharply pointed tips with fusible web. The heart on the right with a turned-edge has a point slightly narrower than a right angle. The bulk of the fabric on the wrong side makes it more difficult to create sharp points.

After working through the two basic techniques of preparation the fun begins. Experiment with stitches and threads, stitching and writing notes directly on the background fabric to create a stitch reference piece. The basic stitches for machine appliqué—straight, zigzag, and blind hem—are found on all machines. If your machine has other programmed stitches (my newest machine has 108), a bonus section is included in Lesson 7 for using some of these decorative stitches.

Lesson 9 walks you through a machine appliquéd project, beginning with fabric selection. The project is 10" square, just right for practicing appliqué techniques, bias stems, and stitching. The book has four projects designed to use all the lessons. I have even included ideas for adding appliqué to purchased items—great when you need a quick gift. Throughout the book you will find quilts to inspire you to move ahead with your appliqué skills. These are from my pattern company Garden Trellis Designs, www.gardentrellisdesigns.com. For information about the beading on the quilts, refer to my other books, Appliqué The basics & beyond and Colorful Quilts for Playful Kids .

Have fun!

Janet Pittman

Lesson
one
Equipment & Supplies

What you need to know about equipment & supplies

Machine appliqué has most of its equipment in common with all quilting, but a few items are unique to the technique. The following items are the ones I find most useful. After reviewing the information decide what you would like to practice and purchase the best equipment and supplies you can afford. It is also a good idea to check with friends who do machine appliqué and get their recommendations.

Sewing Machine Features

For machine appliqué, a sewing machine with zigzag capabilities is a must. Keep your machine clear of lint, oil it regularly, and have it serviced as recommended by the manufacturer. I find the following features helpful:

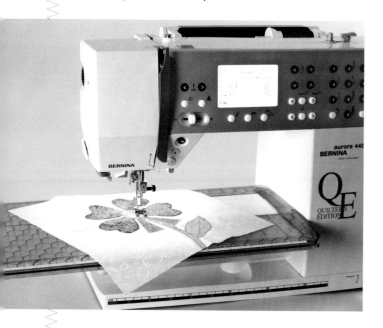

Top Tension: An adjustable upper thread tension makes it easy to get the proper balance between top and bottom tension when using different thread weights and fiber content.

Stitch Width and Length: An adjustable stitch width and length allows you to make choices in your zigzag stitches, blanket stitch, blind hem stitch, and programmed stitches.

Speed Adjustment: A machine speed adjustment option is especially useful when learning to stitch points and around curves.

Throat Plate: If your machine has an extra-wide throat plate (9mm), you may want to purchase a plate with a smaller opening (5mm). Your narrow zigzag stitches will be more perfect and there will be less puckering.

Needle Position: A needle up/needle down function allows you to leave the needle down at the end of a stitch and gradually pivot or change direction without the appliqué slipping out of place. An adjustable needle position (right or left of center) allows you to move the needle, if necessary, to find the best combination for each stitch and presser foot.

Presser Feet

Most machines come with a selection of presser feet. You may want to add the following feet if you do not have them:

Open-Toe Embroidery or Appliqué Foot:

An open-toe embroidery or appliqué foot has a wide opening in front so you can see where you are stitching. It also has a groove molded in the bottom to allow the build up of thread from stitching to pass under it smoothly. Some machines have a clear plastic foot with a wide slot opening for the needle but are not open in the front. These make the stitches correctly, but do not allow you to see the stitching as you are sewing.

Edge-Stitch Foot:

The edge-stitch foot has a metal flange that moves along the edge of the appliqué allowing blanket stitches to be sewn accurately.

Darning or Free-Motion Foot:

A darning foot, which allows the free moving of material under the foot, is necessary for free-motion stitching. This is the same foot you would use for free-motion quilting. Two of the many styles are shown here.

Machine Needles

Machine needles come in a variety of sizes and designs. Purchase quality needles and replace when they become dull or have a burr on the point.

Machine needles are manufactured for specific uses and their names are an indication of that use. They vary in sharpness of the point, size of the eye, the shape of the groove and thickness of the blade.

Select the smallest needle with the appropriate point for your project. For most machine appliqué with 40- to 60-weight cotton, rayon, or polyester thread on standard quilting cotton, I use a sharp (130 H-M) in size 70/10 or 80/12. For heavier thread use a size 90/14. A top stitch needle (130 N) has an extra long eye for straight lines and even stitches when using heavier thread. For metallic thread use

a 130 MET. An embroidery needle (130 H-E) has a sharper point and a special groove designed for decorative thread. If your project has a heavy weight background or appliqué fabric use a larger needle, even if your thread is not heavy.

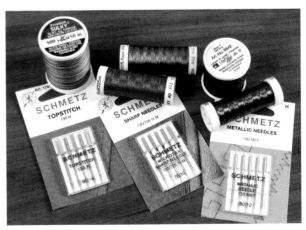

Irons

Use a full-size iron to prepare your background and work with larger machine appliqué pieces. A medium- or travel-size iron is helpful when turning under edges of appliqué. Keep your iron clean from the residue of fusible web. My favorite iron has a nonstick coating which makes cleaning easier.

Scissors

Scissors are designed for different uses. The sharpest ones have knife- or serrated-blade edges. For a lot of continuous cutting I like scissors with a soft handle grip or a spring release. A pair of small, sharp-pointed scissors is helpful for cutting small pieces and clipping curves. Small curved-tip scissors are helpful for clipping threads from the right side of stitched appliqué. I don't cut regular paper with my good scissors, but the paper on fusible webbing is very light weight so I use my smaller, very sharp scissors for this task.

Fusible Web

Paper-backed fusible web is a quick way to get your appliqué pieces temporarily on a background fabric. Trace a pattern directly onto the paper backing, fuse to the wrong side of fabric, cut out the pattern, remove paper, and fuse to the background fabric. Now, you are ready to stitch by machine. It is important to follow manufacturer's instructions for iron temperature and pressing times.

Test several brands to find the one you like. Temperature and time requirements for pressing differ among brands. There are also varying thicknesses of adhesive on the paper, which are designed for different purposes. For machine appliqué I like to use paper-backed fusible web with a light layer of adhesive and a pressing temperature of cotton.

Stabilizers

Stabilizers are essential for many machine appliqué techniques. The thin layer of adhesive in fusible web acts as a stabilizer for fine zigzag stitching, but for wider stitches and stitching through only one or two layers of fabric use a temporary stabilizer. Temporary stabilizers come in sheets or rolls and can be carefully torn, cut, ironed, or washed away after stitching. I like to use lightweight tear-away stabilizer. Extra wide zigzag stitching requires extra stabilizing.

Template Materials

Freezer paper is used for turned-edge appliqué preparation. Heat-resistant template plastic can be used for making circles or other appliqué shapes.

Overlay Materials

For appliqué designs with many layers, I like to prepare an overlay to help with placement of the appliqué pieces. Trace the design onto tracing or tissue paper, lightweight clear vinyl, or clear plastic sheet protectors. Refer to Lesson 5 on pages 40 and 44 for information on using an overlay to arrange appliqué pieces.

Nonstick Pressing Sheets

When working with paper-backed fusible web, I like to use a nonstick coated woven pressing sheet or baking parchment paper both under and on top of the appliqué. This prevents my iron and ironing board from getting sticky with adhesive. You can also pin a piece of muslin to the ironing surface and discard it as it gets sticky. It is helpful if the pressing sheet is slightly transparent so you can see a layout through it. This allows you to fuse all or part of an appliqué motif.

Marking Tools

Marking tools come in many varieties and are selected for a specific use. My favorite is an ultra-fine tip permanent marker that can be used on paper-backed fusible web and template materials and will not smudge when it dries. A mechanical pencil can be used on paper, template materials, and many fabrics, but may smudge or rub off onto fabrics.

Stiletto

A stiletto is very useful when machine stitching to control the points of appliqué and guide fabric when piecing. Stilettos come in metal and bamboo. I often use a seam ripper as a stiletto.

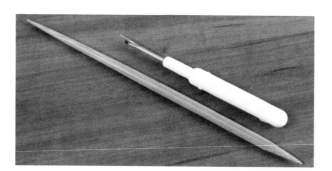

Fabric Glue

Look for water soluble glue sticks to temporarily hold the fabric's folded over edge for turned-edge appliqué.

Pins

Purchase the best pins you can afford. Pins with sharp points and a metal that will not rust are important. I like to use glass-heads on pins that will not melt if ironed.

Light

Good light is essential for machine appliqué. Add extra light in the front and back of your sewing machine to eliminate shadows. There are several styles of lamps with full-spectrum, true-color light bulbs.

Appliqué Inspirations

GARDEN GEMS

Lesson two
Fabric & Thread

What you need to know about fabric & thread

One of the things I enjoy most about machine appliqué is the wide variety of cotton fabrics available in local quilt shops and fabric stores. The color, print, and thread count choices are abundant. Any cotton fabric used for piecing can be used for appliqué. Fabrics with other types of fiber content and weight can be used for machine appliqué but use quilting cottons as you work through the lessons in this book.

Fabric

Thread count is the number of yarns per inch in both the crosswise and lengthwise directions of a piece of fabric. For many projects the thread count is not as important as the color. For fused appliqué or appliqué with turned under edges, fabric with a high thread count, such as batik, does not fray and keeps a crisp edge. If using a very low thread count background fabric with very high thread count appliqué pieces, the background may pucker when the appliqué is machine stitched.

If your project is going to be washed, test the fabrics for colorfastness. If one fabric is prewashed, then all fabrics should be prewashed. Iron all fabrics before using for appliqué. Do not spray with starch or sizing as this may prevent fusible web or freezer paper from adhering to the fabric.

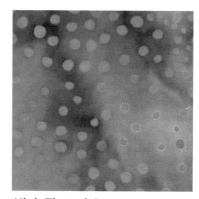
High Thread Count

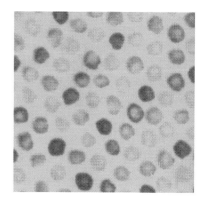
Low Thread Count

High Thread Count

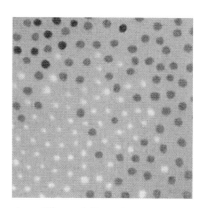
Low Thread Count

When selecting fabrics for an appliqué project, look for contrast in value (light to dark) as well as color. For most appliqué pieces, select hand-dyed or slightly mottled looking prints, tone-on-tone prints, or solids. These will add texture to your quilt without having a pattern getting in the way of the shape of the appliqué pieces. A few prints, especially for larger pieces, can make the appliqué more interesting and even suggest reality.

Contrast in Value
Medium & Dark

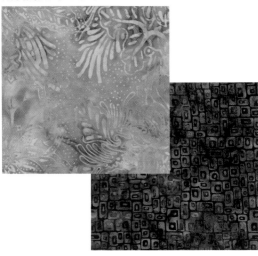

Contrast in Value
Light & Dark

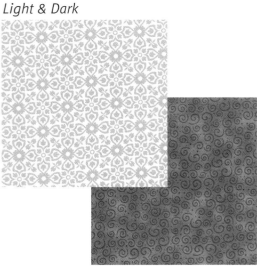

Textured Prints
Mottled & Tone-on-Tone

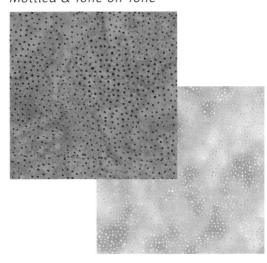

Large Scale Prints

tip:

After mastering the basics of machine appliqué with cotton, there are many other types of fabric that can be used. Heavier weight cottons, as well as silks, polyesters, and rayons, will have different stitching and care requirements. For wallhangings or quilts that will not be washed, any fabric can be used. Make a sample with each fabric to find which method of appliqué works best. Test the method, thread, needles, and stitches.

Dyed Gauze

Krinkle Polyester

Cotton Metallic Blend

Silk & Cotton Blend

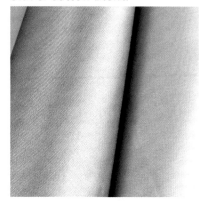

Dupioni Silk

Upholstery Fabric

Thread

The wide variety of thread colors, textures, and fibers that are available is another thing I enjoy about machine appliqué. Thread spools are usually marked with the fiber content, size, and ply of the thread. The higher the size number, the thinner the thread. The ply number indicates the number of fine yarns that are twisted together.

Cotton thread comes in a wide array of colors making it easy to match almost any appliqué fabric. For normal machine appliqué techniques, I recommend 60/2 or 50/3 embroidery thread. For heavier stitching, I use 40-, 30-, or 12-weight thread.

Monofilament nylon or polyester threads are size .004mm and are usually labeled "invisible". This thread is used for the invisible machine appliqué stitching on page 62. You may already have this thread on hand for invisible machine quilting. The sheen of the thread varies by brand and fiber so experiment to find the look you prefer.

Rayon and polyester threads often have more luster than cotton and therefore are more decorative. The luster or sheen allows the threads to blend well with more shades of appliqué fabric. They also do not appear to have the defined edge cotton thread has after stitching. For basic machine appliqué use 40- to 30-weight rayon or polyester thread. Man-made fibers also come in decorative threads such as metallic and ribbon-like polyester film.

There are a variety of thread choices to use in the bobbin. It is easiest when working with 60/2 or 50/3 embroidery cotton threads to match the bobbin thread to the top thread. You should not have to adjust your machine's top tension to get a perfect looking stitch. If you will be changing top thread color frequently, it is more convenient to choose one color thread for the bobbin. I like to use a polyester 80/2 to 120/2 bobbin thread. The top tension may need to be adjusted so none of the bobbin thread shows on top of your project. For satin zigzag stitching where there is a heavy build up of thread, a fine-weight bobbin thread works best.

Because these threads are so thin, you may have to lower the top tension almost to "0". Don't be afraid to lower the top tension. It is easy to readjust back to normal since most machines have numbers and an indication of a normal balanced tension.

Lesson three

Preparing Fused Appliqué

What you need to know about preparing fused appliqué

The fused appliqué method uses paper-backed fusible web to transfer the pattern to the appliqué fabric and make it adhere to the background fabric. I use this method most often because it is quickest and works especially well for pieces with intricate edges that would be difficult to turn under. A fine zigzag, satin zigzag, and blanket stitch are frequently used on the fused edges. An explanation of these stitches may be found in Lesson 7 on pages 56-61.

Getting Started

1. The patterns in this book are printed in reverse because in the process of using paper-backed fusible web the design is flipped.

   > **NOTE:** Appliqué patterns and motifs in some patterns, books, and magazines are not reversed. In these cases you must decide if you want a reversed motif or need to reverse the pattern before tracing it to fusible web. Symmetrical motifs do not need to be reversed but letters and numbers do.

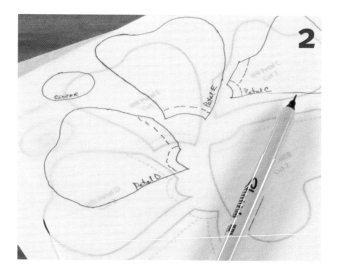

2. Many patterns have two or more pieces fused together to form a motif. Most of the patterns in this book have a dashed line to indicate where one appliqué piece will be placed under another. Trace the solid outline and, if desired, any dashed lines for further reference.

3. The butterfly motifs on page 112 as well as appliqué motifs in many books, magazines, and patterns are shown as a complete motif and you will need to make your own underlap lines. Trace a dashed line on any edges where one appliqué piece will be placed under another piece. Mark a 1/4" extension to that side of the pattern.

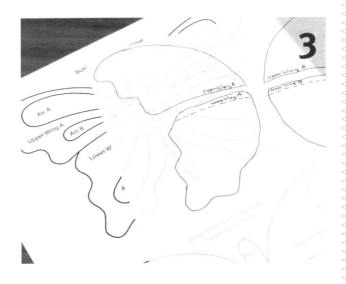

Preparing Appliqué Pieces

1. Place lightweight paper-backed fusible web paper-side up on the appliqué pattern. Using an ultra-fine tip permanent marker or pencil, trace each pattern piece onto the paper side of the fusible web. If a pattern piece will be placed under another, mark extensions with dashed lines.

2. Mark the pattern name or number near an edge of the pattern. This is for reference when building the appliqué designs.

3. Cut away excess fusible web approximately 1/4" outside the traced lines. Excess fusible web wastes fabric and makes it difficult to fuse pieces near each other.

4. If desired, remove the fusible web from the center of the larger pattern pieces. Cut through an edge into the center of the pattern. Cut out the center leaving a scant 1/4" inside the traced line. This makes the fabric center softer to the touch and in appearance. This technique is frequently called "windowing".

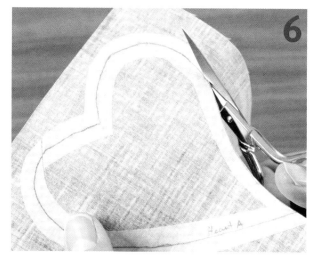

5. Fuse patterns to wrong side of pressed fabric, following manufacturer's directions regarding pressing time and iron temperature.

6. Cut out fused appliqué pieces on the traced line. Do not remove paper backing until just before arranging the pieces on the background fabric. The paper preserves the pattern name or number. If you are working with hand-dyed or batik fabrics where it is hard to tell right from wrong side of fabric, this will remind you which side should be down, preventing a gummed up iron surface.

tips:

Grouping appliqué pieces: Trace appliqué pieces that will be cut from the same fabric about 1/8" apart. This will save fabric.

Fussy cutting: If you want to have a specific printed motif or color shading on an appliqué piece, trace, and fuse the pattern piece separately. Windowing the paper allows you to see the area desired in the appliqué.

Protect your iron and ironing board: To prevent fusible web from gumming up your ironing board and the surface of your iron, cover the appliqué patterns with parchment paper or a nonstick pressing sheet. Do this as you are pressing the fusible web to the wrong side of the appliqué fabric and as you are arranging the layout.

Removing paper backing: If you do not window the fusible web, it may be difficult to find an edge of paper to pull away. Drag a pin across the center of the fused pattern to cut the paper but not the fabric. This creates an edge of paper to pull.

tips:

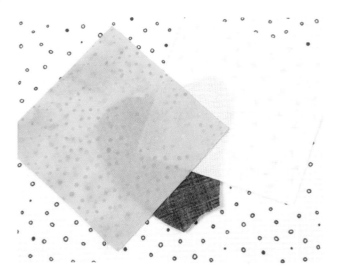

Lining Light Color

When light-colored appliqué pieces overlap darker colors, the darker color often shadows through. To prevent this, line the appliqué pieces with white or the same color fabric. Notice how the area of overlap of the light yellow flower center and white lining fabric does not have a ghost of the rose petal fabric showing through.

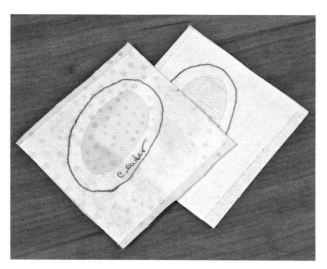

For paper-backed fusible web, make duplicate tracings. Fuse the pattern pieces in the same position on the same size pieces of appliqué and lining fabric. Remove the paper from the appliqué fabric and fuse it to the lining fabric, aligning the patterns and fabric edges.

Cut out using the traced line on the web of the lining fabric.

For turned-edge appliqué, cut out an exact pattern from the lining fabric and insert under the appliqué before stitching.

Getting Started Pattern

Heart A

tip:

Press all appliqué fabrics to remove wrinkles or creases before applying the fusible web. Any creases in the fabric will become permanent when fused. Background fabrics will also need to be pressed.

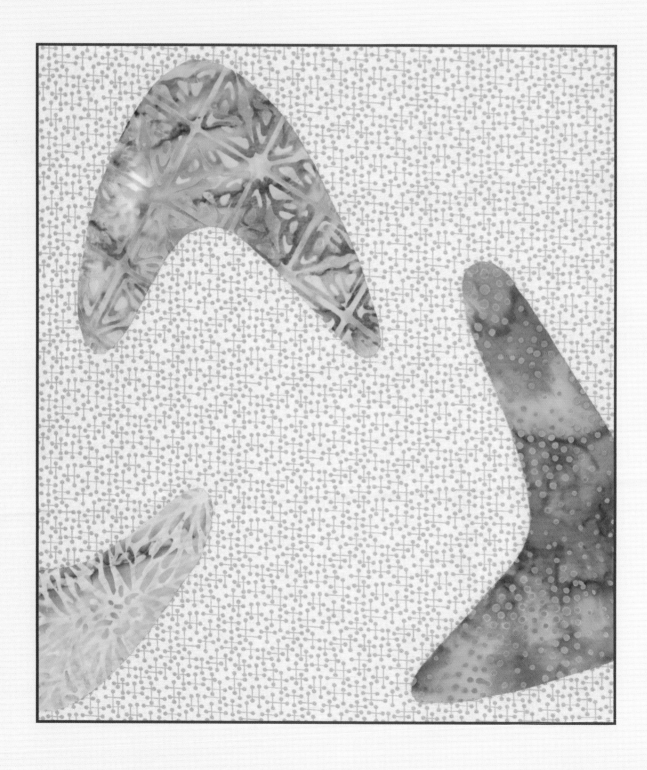

Lesson four

Preparing Turned-Edge Appliqué

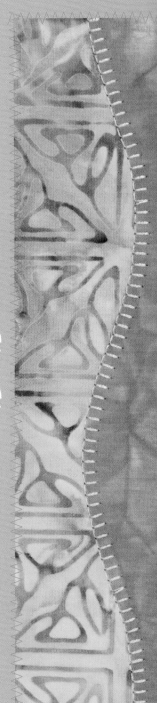

What you need to know about preparing turned-edge appliqué

Turned-edge appliqué pieces have the appearance of traditional appliqué, which I like. Freezer paper is used to create a temporary template as a guide for turning the appliqué edge. Stitch the pieces with invisible stitching for a hand appliquéd look or blanket stitching for a retro look. Zigzag stitching may also be used.

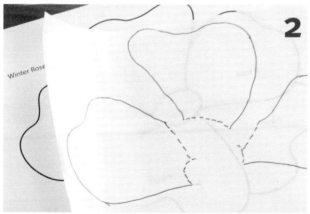

Getting Started

1. The patterns in this book are printed in reverse because in this process of preparing turned-edge appliqué the design is flipped.

2. Many patterns have two or more pieces stitched together to form a motif. Most of the patterns in this book have a dashed line to indicate where one appliqué piece will be placed under another. Trace solid outer lines and any dashed underlap lines.

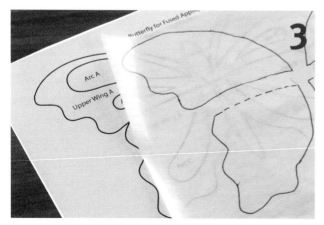

3. The butterfly motifs on page 112 as well as appliqué motifs in many books, magazines, and patterns are shown as a complete motif and you will have to make your own underlap lines. Trace a dashed line on any edges where one appliqué piece will be placed under another piece. The dashed line indicates where you will not turn under the edge.

Preparing Appliqué Pieces using Freezer Paper

1. Place freezer paper <u>shiny</u> side up on the appliqué pattern. Using an ultra-fine point permanent marker, trace each pattern piece. If one pattern piece will be placed under another, mark extensions with dashed lines.

2. Flip the pattern over and mark the pattern name or number on the dull side. This is for reference when building the appliqué designs.

> **NOTE:** *Appliqué patterns and motifs in some patterns, books, and magazines are not reversed. In these cases you must decide if you want a reversed motif or need to reverse the pattern before tracing it to freezer paper. Symmetrical motifs do not need to be reversed but letters and numbers do.*

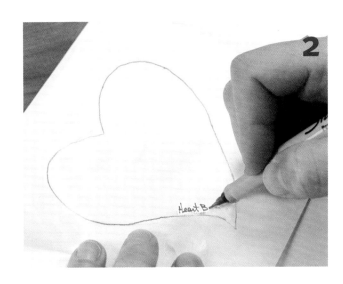

3. Cut the pattern pieces out on the traced line. For pieces with a dashed underlap line, cut just outside the dashed line.

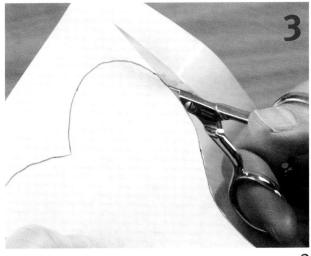

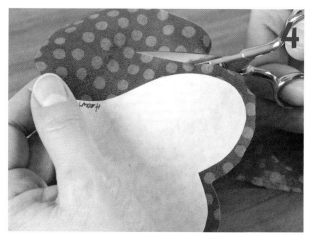

4. Press freezer paper pattern shiny side down on right side of appliqué fabric. Trim fabric a scant 1/4" outside freezer paper pattern. Do not remove paper until just before stitching the pieces to the background fabric. This preserves the pattern name or number.

5. Clip any inside curves around the edge of the appliqué shape. When clipping inside curves, clip approximately halfway to the edge of the pattern. To prevent fraying, make clips on the bias of the fabric. Do not clip on any dashed line underlaps.

6. Clip inside points straight into the point to within one thread of the pattern.

7. Using a washable glue stick, apply glue to the seam allowance edge on the wrong side of the fabric. Do not apply glue to the dashed line underlap sections. To protect the table surface, place appliqué pieces on parchment or freezer paper.

8. Working in small sections, use the edge of the freezer paper as a guide to finger press the glued fabric allowance to the wrong side. Place the tip of your thumb on top and index finger underneath the shapes as you turn the seam allowance. On outside curves make very small tucks or pleats in the fabric. Apply more glue, as necessary. Do not finger press the seam allowance on edges marked with dashed lines.

9. For sharp corners and points, begin by finger pressing the excess fabric at the point directly away from the point. Then, finger press the seam allowance from one edge to the wrong side.

10. Finally, finger press the other side, applying more glue, and trimming seam allowances, if necessary.

33

tips:

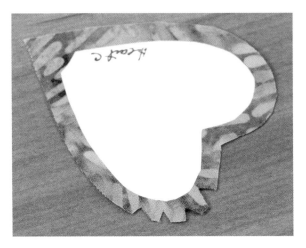

If an outside curve is very pronounced or almost pointed, you may need to make small V-shaped cuts in the seam allowance. The fabric will lay flatter instead of overlapping.

Turning a perfect circle

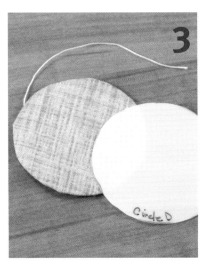

1. Trace a circle on heat resistant plastic template material and cut out. Place the template on the wrong side of the appliqué fabric and trace around the circle. Cut out a scant 1/4" beyond the circle. Knot a short length of thread. Make running stitches between the traced circle and the edge of the fabric.

2. Pull the thread end to gather the seam allowance edges around and over the circle template. Smooth out the gathers. Take a single backstitch to hold thread in place. Firmly press the edges.

3. Loosen the backstitch and the gathering and remove the template. Re-press. The template may be reused.

Preparing Appliqué Pieces using a Faced Technique

Faced appliqué preparation is especially effective for large appliqué pieces with gentle curves and simple shapes. Lightweight interfacing will stay under the appliqué or water soluble stabilizer will dissolve during washing.

1. Use lightweight non-fusible non-woven interfacing or water soluble stabilizer as a facing. Place the facing on your pattern and trace the individual pieces. Mark a dashed line on any edges where the piece will underlap another appliqué piece. Mark the facing with pattern name or number. Pin the marked facing on the right side of a piece of similarly sized appliqué fabric.

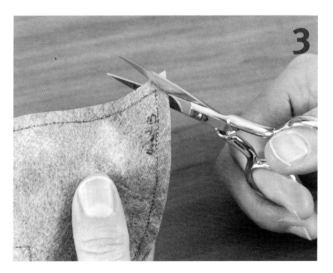

2. Stitch all the way around the pieces on the marked line, using a smaller than normal stitch length. Use a thread color that blends with the appliqué fabric. If the pattern has underlap edges start at one side of the dashed line and stitch around to the other side, leaving an opening where the underlap is located.

3. Trim seam allowance to a scant 1/4". Clip the inside and outside curves around the edge of the appliqué shape approximately halfway to the stitched line. Clip inside points to within one thread of the line. Trim outside points straight across.

4. If stitching has been done all the way around the piece, make a 2" to 3" slit in the center of the facing material. Be careful not to cut through the appliqué fabric.

5. Carefully turn the piece inside out through the slit or unstitched opening.

6. Finger press to smooth out the edges and then press from the right side.

NOTE: *If desired after pressing, trim away most of the facing material leaving the pressed fabric edge. This is especially important if using a water soluble facing.*

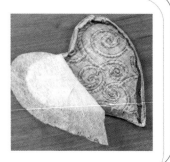

Getting Started Pattern

Heart B

Appliqué Inspirations

SUMMER SUNFLOWERS

Lesson five

Arranging Appliqué

What you need to know about arranging appliqué

After the appliqué pieces are prepared they must be arranged on the project or background. The appliqué projects in this book have been designed to be simple for the learning process, however some require a layout for positioning the pieces.

Getting Started

1. A single appliqué piece or a group of pieces that form a unit are called "motifs".

2. A "layout" is the overall appliqué design. This could be a motif or group of motifs and single pieces. The layouts in this book are full size. Sometimes patterns are reduced in size. If you encounter a pattern that has been reduced, enlarge it by copying it at the percentage listed on the pattern.

3. An "overlay" is a full-size copy of the layout that has been traced with a permanent marker onto tracing or tissue paper, lightweight clear vinyl, or sheet protectors. Tracing paper is used in the step 3 photograph.

4. Some layouts have the center marked with an "+" or a dot. To find the center of your background fabric, fold it in half in both directions. Mark the center with a pin. If the center will be covered with an appliqué, mark it with a pencil.

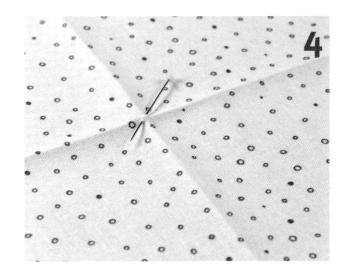

5. To fuse the appliqué pieces or motifs to the background fabric, follow manufacturer's directions for iron temperature and pressing time.

6. To hold the pieces in place for turned edge appliqué insert pins at a right angle to the edge. As you are stitching the edge, remove each pin just before you get to it.

Pre-fusing Appliqué Motifs

1. Place a full-size layout under a nonstick pressing sheet or baking parchment paper. Remove paper backing from the appliqué pieces one at a time. Arrange the pieces on the pressing sheet, starting with the ones closest to the background. Tack in place with the tip of a hot iron.

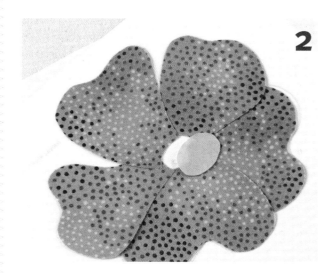

2. Continue adding appliqué pieces and tacking in place with the iron tip to form the motif. Work from the background up. Fuse the entire motif with a hot iron. Let cool and remove the fused motif from the nonstick sheet.

Arranging Motifs and Pieces on Backgrounds

Light Backgrounds

1. If your background is light in value, copy or trace the motif layout to a piece of white paper and position it under the background fabric. Remove paper from the appliqué pieces one at a time. Arrange the pieces on the background beginning with the ones closest to the background. Pin or tack in place with the tip of a hot iron.

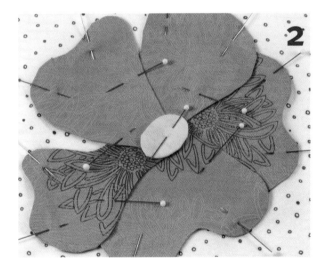

2. Continue pinning or tacking appliqué pieces in place to form the motif. Work from the background up. If using fused appliqué, press the entire motif with a hot iron.

Medium to Dark Backgrounds

1. If your background is dark in value and you are unable to see the printed lines of a layout through it, make a design layout overlay. Cut a piece of overlay material approximately the size of the appliqué background. Place on top of the full-size layout and trace the design. Refer to Lesson 1, page 11 for information on overlay material. The photographs on this page use clear vinyl for the overlay.

2. Position the design overlay on the background and pin to the top or one side. Remove paper from the appliqué pieces. Arrange the appliqué a few at a time on the background by lifting the overlay slightly and placing the pieces. Pin in place and continue adding pieces to form the design.

3. For fused appliqué, remove overlay and tack in place by touching the tip of a hot iron in several places. Remove pins and press the entire motif with a hot iron.

Arranging Simple Appliqué

A simple appliqué or already fused motifs can be positioned directly on light or dark backgrounds according to the layout or placement directions and then pinned or fused in place.

For simple motifs that are centered or arranged symmetrically, divide the area by gently folding the background into quarters and positioning the appliqué.

Appliqué Inspirations

BUTTERFLIES

Lesson SIX

Stitching Basics

What you need to know about machine appliqué stitching

The basic steps for the appliqué stitching shown in these lessons is the same. Practice the set-up, beginning stitching, and ending techniques to make your machine appliqué look like you have been appliquéing for years.

Note: The stitched examples are shown using a contrasting thread color so the process is easier to follow.

Setting Up for Machine Stitching

Most machine stitches for appliqué have the same basic setup.

• Choose a needle that works best for your combination of fabric and thread. Use a smaller needle for finer fabrics, as well as monofilament and finer threads. A larger needle should be used for decorative threads and heavier fabrics. A specialty needle may be needed for some decorative threads.

• Use an open-toe embroidery or appliqué presser foot to clearly see the edges, curves, and points of the appliqué pieces as you stitch. These feet have a wide opening in front of the stitches and a groove on the underside to accommodate the buildup of thread. See the photo in Lesson 1 on page 9.

• Choose a bobbin thread that best suits your top thread and fabrics. Review the bobbin thread information in Lesson 2 on page 19.

• Position the presser foot for the zigzag, blanket, or invisible stitch so the right swing of the needle will be next to the outside edge of the appliqué piece and the left swing of the needle will come onto the appliqué.

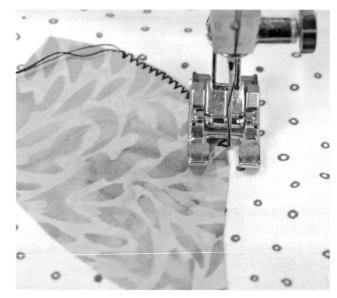

Beginning and Ending Stitching

Beginning Stitching

1. When beginning the stitching, bring the bobbin thread to the top. Take one stitch and pull on the top thread to bring the bobbin thread loop up.

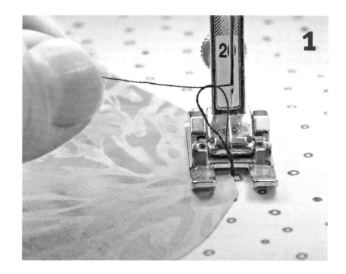

2. Pull on the loop of bobbin thread to bring the tail to the top. Bringing the bobbin thread to the top will prevent a snarl or knot of thread on the back of your appliqué.

3. Take a few locking stitches, short straight stitches very close together, and proceed with edge-stitching.

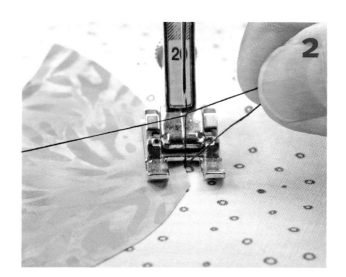

Ending Stitching When Using Matching Thread

At the end of the edge-stitching, take a few very short straight stitches to lock the threads. Pull appliqué away from the needle. Clip beginning and ending thread tails.

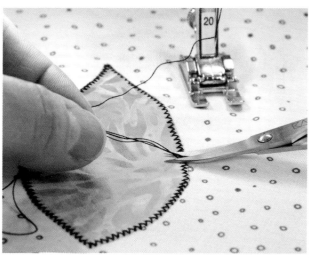

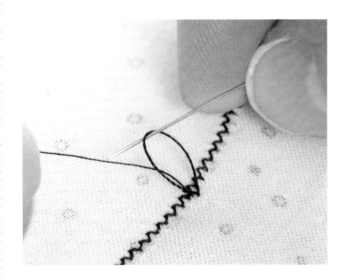

Ending Stitching When Using Contrasting Thread

When using thread that contrasts in either color or value, you can use the steps already given or for a cleaner look pull the threads to the back. Do not take the small locking stitches. Leave 6" tails of thread at both the beginning and ending stitching. Pull top thread through to the back and tie a knot. If the knot does not seem to hold, affix with permanent fabric glue.

Appliqué Inspirations

GREEN BUGS

Stabilizing for Machine Stitching

It is often necessary to stabilize appliqué pieces to prevent puckering when:

- using stitches that make wide zigzags or swings of the needle.
- stitching a bias edge, such as curves or circles.
- stitching in an area where the stitch zigs away from the appliqué fabric into the background or a single thickness of fabric.

If you are stitching on fused or turned under edges with a narrow zigzag or blanket stitch you will probably not need to stabilize the stitching.

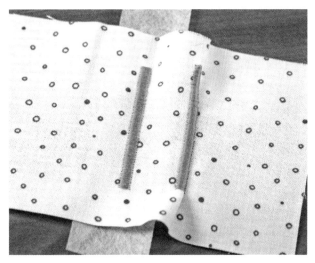

The stitch sample above shows puckering on the right line of satin zigzag stitching where there was no stabilizer. To stabilize stitching, place a piece of stabilizer under the appliqué. For very heavy stitching you may need a couple of thicknesses of stabilizer. Carefully tear or cut away the stabilizer after stitching. Refer to Lesson 1, page 11 for information on stabilizers.

tip:

I like to use a stiletto or the tip of a seam ripper to hold down a turned-edge point if it has become loose.

Lesson seven
Looking at Stitches

What you need to know about stitches

This lesson covers several basic machine appliqué stitches—satin zigzag, fine zigzag, blanket, blind hem—and an overview for using decorative stitches to add texture and color to your projects. The best way I know to improve appliqué stitching is to make stitch samples. Use your background and appliqué fabrics to test stitches, threads, tension, and stabilizers.

Note: The stitched examples are shown using a contrasting thread color so the process is easier to follow.

Making Stitch Samples

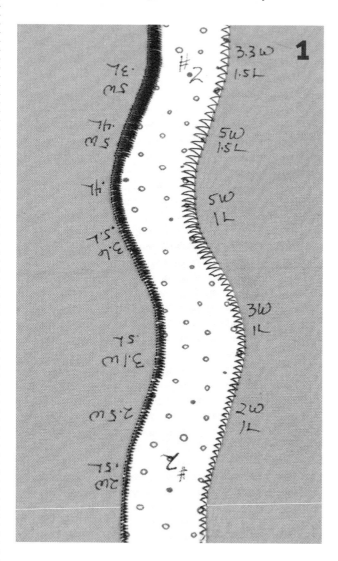

1. As you go through this lesson make a sample of each stitch you would like to use. Cut straight or curved strips of fused fabric or press under the edges and apply to a neutral background. Vary the widths and lengths of the stitches within the lesson. Mark the stitch length and width on the background next to the appliqué piece.

2. Cut out an extra appliqué motif of each fabric color you will be using. Or, use the scraps cut away from fused motifs. Fuse or pin the motifs to a piece of the background fabric.

3. Test the threads and stitch widths and lengths until you find a combination you like. Mark the stitch length and width on the background next to the appliqué piece.

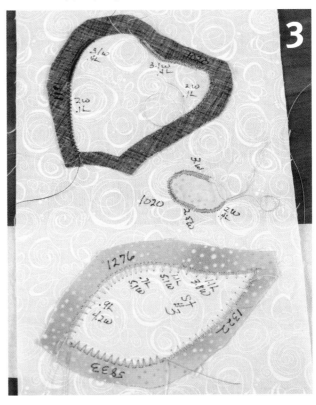

tip:

Adjust the tension, if necessary, for each combination of top and bobbin thread. Keep testing every time you change one or the other.

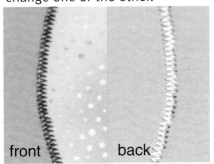

This tension is correct for a zigzag stitch. There is a very small bit of top thread coming through to the back. This makes nice V points on the front.

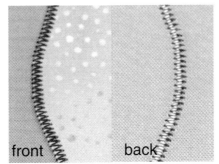

When there is too much top thread showing on the back, the top tension is too loose. Adjust the top tension to a higher number.

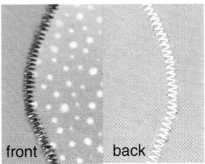

The top tension is too tight. This causes the zigzags to have curved edges instead of clean Vs because the bobbin thread is showing on the front. Adjust the top tension to a lower number.

Satin Zigzag Stitches

Satin zigzag stitches can be narrow to wide and are spaced close together to make a solid line. This stitch is most frequently used for fused appliqué but can also be stitched along the edge of turned-edge appliqué. A satin zigzag stitch is more decorative than a fine zigzag stitch (page 58). If stitched in a contrasting value or color it will stand out and give the appliqué piece an outlined look. Satin zigzag stitching will hold up to regular washing and drying.

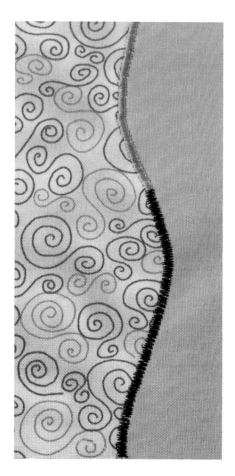

Stitching Instructions

- The satin zigzag stitch should secure just the edge of the appliqué. I usually use 40-weight rayon or polyester or 60-weight cotton embroidery thread in a matching or contrasting color.

- Satin zigzag is stitched about 2mm to 3mm-wide and at a satin setting (.4mm to .3mm-long). The length of the stitch depends on the weight of the thread. Thinner thread will need to have a shorter length.

- Position the presser foot so the right swing of the stitch will be next to the edge of the appliqué. The left swing of the needle will then come onto the appliqué. Begin stitching at the junction of two pieces or along a continuous edge.

- The stitch can be made up to 5mm-wide, but be sure to make a practice test at this width and add stabilizer if necessary.

- Practice the special stitching directions for curves, corners and points, reducing machine speed for more control.

Stitching Curves

Outside Curves

When stitching outside curves, occasionally pivot the appliqué. Stop with the needle down on the right swing, raise the presser foot, and pivot the appliqué slightly, lower the presser foot, and continue stitching. The tightness of the curve will dictate how often you need to pivot. If you pivot with the needle down on the left swing, there will be gaps in the stitches.

Inside Curves

When stitching inside curves, occasionally pivot the appliqué. Stop with the needle down on the left swing, raise the presser foot, and pivot the appliqué slightly, lower the presser foot, and continue stitching. The tightness of the curve will dictate how often you need to pivot. If you pivot with the needle down on the right swing, there will be gaps in the stitches on the appliqué.

Stitching Corners and Points

Outside Corners

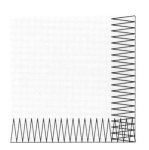

To stitch an outside corner, stitch to the end of the appliqué and stop with the needle down on the right edge. Raise the presser foot, pivot the fabric, lining up with the next side, lower the presser foot, and continue stitching. You may have to adjust the presser foot and needle position after you turn the corner to realign with the edge.

Inside Corners

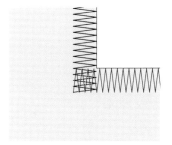

An inside corner is stitched by stitching past the corner the width of the stitch. Stop with needle down on the left side. Raise the presser foot and pivot the fabric lining up with the next edge. Lower the presser foot and continue stitching. If the corner is less than 90-degrees, move the fabric slightly so the first right stitch is within the previous stitches.

Tapered Points

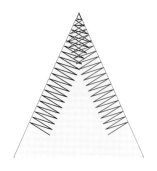

Move the needle position to the far right. Stitch to the place near the point on the appliqué where the left swing touches the next side. Gradually decrease the stitch width, stitching to the point. Stop with the needle down on the right edge. Raise the presser foot and pivot the fabric, lining up with the next side. Lower the presser foot and stitching slowly, gradually increase the stitch width to the original setting—this may be several stitches. Continue stitching.

Fine Zigzag Stitches

Fine zigzag stitches are usually narrow in width and when stitched with a fine, matching thread will almost disappear. This stitch is most frequently used for fused appliqué but can also be stitched along the edge of turned-edge appliqué. Fine zigzag stitching will hold up to gentle washing and drying.

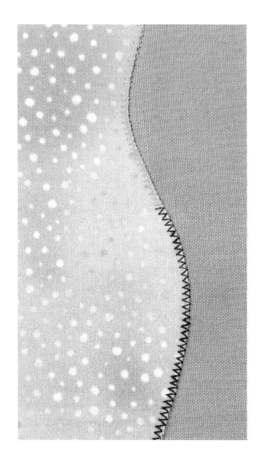

Stitching Instructions

- The fine zigzag stitch should secure just the edge of the appliqué. I usually use 40-weight rayon or polyester or 60-weight cotton embroidery thread in a matching color.

- The fine zigzag is stitched approximately 1.8mm to 2mm-wide and about .8mm-long.

- Position the presser foot so the right swing of the stitch will be next to the edge of the appliqué. The left swing of the needle will then come onto the appliqué. Begin stitching at the junction of two pieces or along a continuous edge.

- Practice the special stitching directions for curves, corners, and points, reducing machine speed for more control.

tip:

Avoiding Frayed Edges

If the right swing of the fine or satin zigzag stitch is on the appliqué rather than just over the edge, it may cause fraying, especially on a loosely woven fabric.

Stitching Curves

Outside Curves

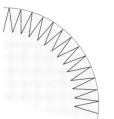

When stitching outside curves, occasionally pivot the appliqué. Stop with the needle down on the right swing, raise the presser foot, and pivot the appliqué slightly, lower the presser foot, and continue stitching. The tightness of the curve will dictate how often you need to pivot. If you pivot with the needle down on the left swing, there will be gaps in the stitches.

Inside Curves

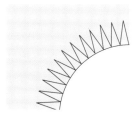

When stitching inside curves, occasionally pivot the appliqué. Stop with the needle down on the left swing, raise the presser foot, and pivot the appliqué slightly, lower the presser foot, and continue stitching. The tightness of the curve will dictate how often you need to pivot. If you pivot with the needle down on the right swing, there will be gaps in the stitches on the appliqué.

Stitching Corners and Points

Outside Corners

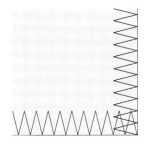

To stitch an outside corner, stitch to the end of the appliqué and stop with the needle down on the right edge. Raise the presser foot, pivot the fabric, lining up with the next side, lower the presser foot, and continue stitching. You may have to adjust the presser foot and needle position after you turn the corner.

Inside Corners

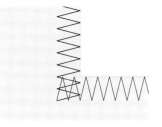

An inside corner is stitched by stitching past the corner the width of the stitch. Stop with needle down on the left side. Raise the presser foot and pivot the fabric lining up with the next edge. Lower the presser foot and continue stitching. If the corner is less than 90-degrees, move the fabric slightly so the first right stitch is within the previous stitches.

Tapered Points

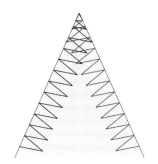

For a tapered point stitch to the end of the appliqué corner, decreasing the stitch width the last few stitches, and stopping with the needle down on the right edge. Raise the presser foot and pivot the fabric, lining up with the next side. Lower the presser foot, take one stitch, then gradually increase the stitch width until the stitching is at the original setting—this will only be a few stitches. Continue stitching.

Blanket Stitch

The blanket, or buttonhole, stitch can be used with fused edge or with turned edge appliqué. The blanket stitch gives a crisp look to the edges of appliqué and is used to mimic broiderie perse and other hand stitched appliqué such as Sunbonnet Sue.

Stitching Instructions

- Threads used most often for the blanket stitch are 50- or heavier weight black or contrasting colored cotton thread.

- The blanket stitch is a programmed stitch on most sewing machines. There may be more than one variation so make a test sample to get the best variation for your project. Make a stitch sample and test various widths, lengths, and weights of thread to achieve the look you want.

- Use an edge stitch presser foot, if you have one, to help guide the presser foot next to the edge of the appliqué.

- Position the presser foot so the forward stitches of the blanket stitch are along the right edge of the appliqué but not so close that they are hidden by the appliqué edge. The left swing of the needle will then come onto the appliqué. Begin stitching at the junction of two pieces or along a continuous line. It is more difficult to start at an inner or outer point.

- Practice the special stitching directions for curves, corners, and points, reducing machine speed for more control.

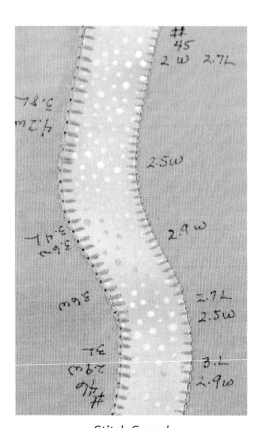

Stitch Sample

Stitching Curves

Outside Curves

When stitching outside curves, occasionally pivot the appliqué. Stop with the needle down at the end of a forward stitch, raise the presser foot, and pivot the appliqué slightly, lower the presser foot,and continue stitching. The tightness of the curve will dictate how often you need to pivot. If you pivot with the needle down on the left swing, there will be gaps in the swing stitches.

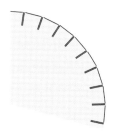

Inside Curves

When stitching inside curves, occasionally pivot the appliqué. Stop with the needle down at the end of a forward stitch, raise the presser foot, and pivot the appliqué slightly, lower the presser foot, and continue stitching. The tightness of the curve will dictate how often you need to pivot. If you pivot with the needle down on the left swing, there will be crossovers in the swing stitches.

Stitching Corners

Outside Corners

For an outside corner, stitch to the corner of the appliqué, stopping with the needle down at the end of a forward stitch. You may need to adjust the fabric or stitch length as you approach the corner to get the completed forward stitch exactly at the corner. Raise the presser foot and pivot the fabric 45-degrees. Lower the presser foot and complete a swing to the left and back. Raise the presser foot and pivot the fabric another 45-degrees, lining up with the next edge. Lower the presser foot and continue stitching.

Inside Corners

For an inside corner, stitch to the corner of the appliqué stopping with needle down at the end of a swing stitch. Raise the presser foot and pivot the fabric 45-degrees. Lower the presser foot, lower the feed dogs, and make the next "forward" stitch, holding the fabric so the needle goes in the same hole. Make a swing stitch. Make the forward stitch, again holding the fabric so the needle goes in the same hole. Raise the presser foot, pivot the fabric 45-degrees, lower the presser foot, raise the feed dogs, and continue stitching.

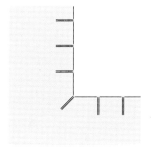

Tapered Points

Tapered points are stitched in the same manner as the outside corners. Make the first pivot to divide the corner in half. You may need to shorten the stitch width for one stitch so the swing stitches do not overlap each other.

Blind Hem – invisible machine stitch

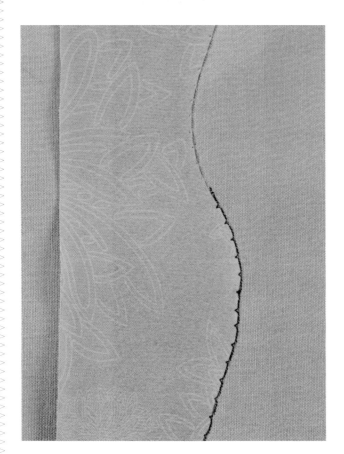

The blind hem stitch, which is found on most machines, is recommended for turned edge appliqué to give the look and feel of hand appliqué. A very small blanket stitch will achieve this same invisible appearance.

Stitching Instructions

- The top thread should be invisible monofilament nylon or polyester thread or 60-weight cotton or silk thread in a color that matches the appliqué fabric exactly. In the bobbin use 60-weight cotton or polyester thread in a color that matches the appliqué background.

- In most instances a 1mm-wide and .7mm-long stitch will work best. There should be 1/8" to 1/4" between bites (left swing of the needle), and each bite should catch one or two threads of the appliqué piece. Since machines vary, make a stitch sample and test various widths and lengths to achieve an invisible hand appliqué look.

- The blind hem stitch has two to four straight forward stitches and one zigzag stitch to the left. Position the presser foot so the forward stitches are along the edge of the appliqué and the zigzag stitch will catch one to two threads of the appliqué. Begin stitching at the junction of two pieces or anywhere on a continuous line.

- Practice the special stitching directions for curves, corners, and points, reducing machine speed for more control.

Stitching Corners and Curves

Outside Corners and Tapered Points

The outside corner is stitched by stitching to the corner of the appliqué and stopping with the needle down at the end of the  forward stitches. Raise the presser foot and pivot the fabric dividing the corner in half. Lower the presser foot and complete a zigzag stitch. Raise the presser foot and pivot the fabric lining up with the next edge. Lower the presser foot and continue stitching.

Inside Corners

An inside corner is stitched by stitching to the corner of the appliqué and stopping with the needle down at the end of the forward stitches. Raise 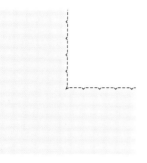 the presser foot and pivot the fabric 45-degrees. Lower the presser foot and complete a zigzag stitch in the crotch of the corner. Raise the presser foot and pivot the fabric another 45-degrees lining up with the next edge. Lower the presser foot and continue stitching.

Stitching Curves

No special consideration has to be given to the curves because the width and length of the stitches is so small. Gradually turn the project as you go around curves keeping the forward stitches next to the edge of the appliqué.

Appliqué Inspirations

NAPTIME ANIMALS

What you need to know about decorative stitching

For an extra decorative touch, I love using free-motion straight stitching and the programmed stitches found on most sewing machines. Use these stitches with contrasting or decorative thread to show off the stitching and add definition to the appliqué.

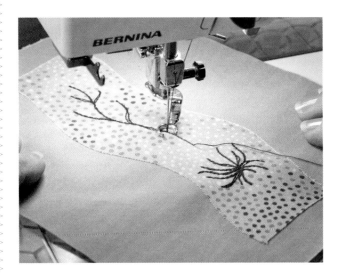

Free-motion Straight Stitching

Free-motion straight stitching is very versatile and can be used for leaf veins, flower centers, or circles. Set up your machine by dropping the feed dogs and using a darning or free-motion presser foot. When I am doing concentrated stitching, such as a flower center, I add a piece of stabilizer under the section.

Stitch free-motion curved lines to make the center of a rose. Use two or three values of yellow to give added realism.

Free-motion stitch lines to mimic the curve of the center vein of leaves. Add side veins on larger leaves.

Utility Stitches

Utility stitches on most sewing machines are designed for clothing construction and repair. But, you can use them for decoration. They are the lowest numbered stitches on your machine after straight and zigzag. Make a test sample of several as reference, marking the stitch number beside each sewn line.

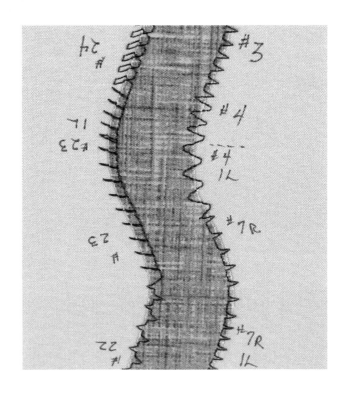

The rose leaf edge is stitched with a blind hem or vari-overlock stitch. The zig out into the background gives the leaf a notched edge. Add a sheet of stabilizer to prevent puckering around the edges.

Use the triple straight stitch to create a heavy vein line. By stitching forward, back, and then forward again, even a 60-weight cotton or 40-weight rayon appears thick. When stitching curves make all direction changes by pivoting at at the beginning of the triple sequence. This stitch also needs stabilizing.

Satin Programmed Stitches

The programmed decorative stitch patterns on your machine can add texture and interest to machine appliqué. The stitches vary by machine, so yours may be different than those shown here. I have separated them into satin and non-satin stitch categories. Both are fun to use.

Make a test sample of several from each category as reference, marking the stitch number beside each sewn line.

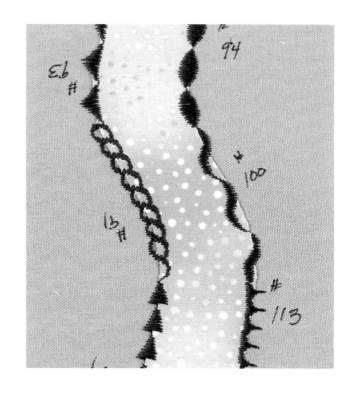

I like to use a satin programmed stitch I call "football" to add definition to the appliqué edge between patterned fabrics.

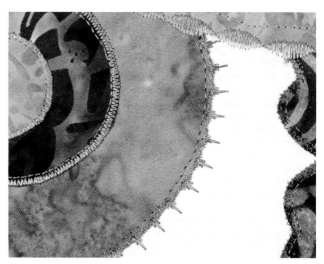

The satin programmed stitch I call "crown" has a point. I have used it here to add a spoke-like texture to the circles. I also like to use this stitch around animals for a spiky fur texture.

Non-Satin Programmed Stitches

Make a test sample of several non-satin programmed stitches as reference, marking the stitch number beside each sewn line.

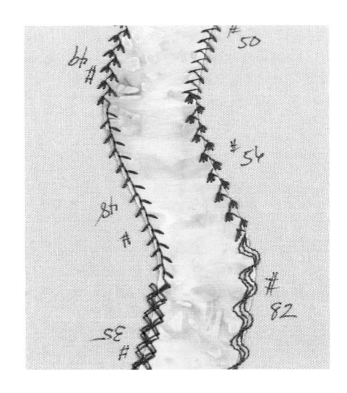

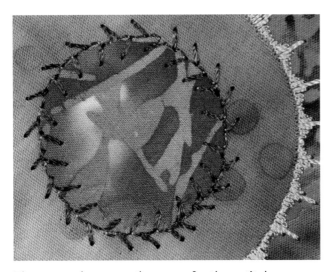

There may be more than one feather stitch on your machine. In the example, I have used a single feather stitch around a circle to give texture.

A feather stitch is also a good alternate stitch to give a notched edge to rose and sunflower leaves. In the example, I have used a decorative triple feather.

Lesson
eight
Preparing Bias Stems

What you need to know about preparing bias stems

I love the softness a curved stem gives an appliquéd piece. Fabric for curved stems needs to be cut on the bias. This allows the stem to curve smoothly without tucks or puckers. There are many methods for making bias stems, but the following two are most often used. Both start with finding the bias of your fabric.

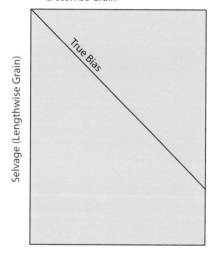

Crosswise Grain

True Bias

Selvage (Lengthwise Grain)

Finding the True Bias

The diagram shows the lengthwise and crosswise grain edges of the fabric. The fabric's true bias is the line half way between the two. The lengthwise grain is along the selvage edge which is the non-cut edge where the fabric name and manufacturer is generally printed. The crosswise grain is the edge where the fabric has been cut when purchased. On a fat-quarter, the lengthwise grain is the 18" length while the crosswise grain will range from 20" to 22".

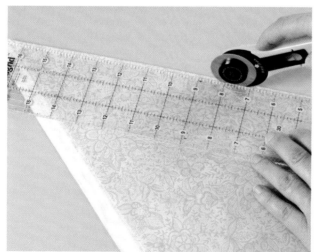

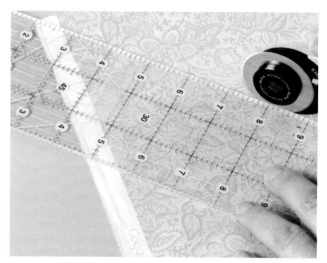

Trim fabric on the crosswise grain line. Fold the cut edge over to meet the selvage (lengthwise grain). This diagonal fold is the true bias (45-degree). Lay a ruler slightly inside this fold and cut off the fold. The resulting edges can be used for cutting bias strips.

If you prefer, use the 45-degree angle line on your ruler. Place ruler with the 45-degree line along the selvage. Make a cut and then use these edges to cut bias strips.

Bias Stems–Paper-Backed Fusible Web

This method can be used with any appliqué method. Most frequently it is used when the appliqué preparation also uses paper-backed fusible web. This method makes it easy to cut very narrow stems.

1. Find the true bias of the stem fabric. Cut a piece of paper-backed fusible web a little wider than the total measurements of the stems needed and a little longer. Following manufacturer's directions, press the paper-backed fusible web to the wrong side of the stem fabric near the bias edge.

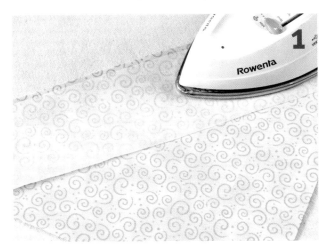

2. Trim off the edge of the fabric and fusible web. Cut stems desired width.

tip:

Tapered Stems

Stems can be cut at a slight angle to make them taper from wide to narrow.

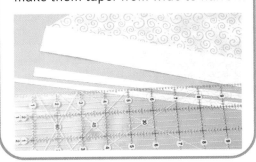

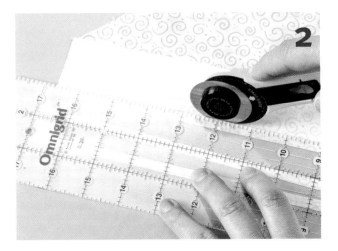

3. Mark the stem position on the appliqué background. Following manufacturer's directions, press bias stem into position over the line and curve as desired.

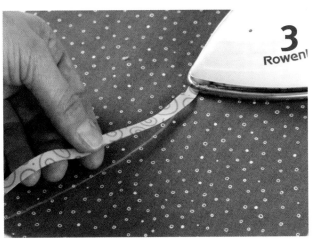

Bias Stems—Triple Fold

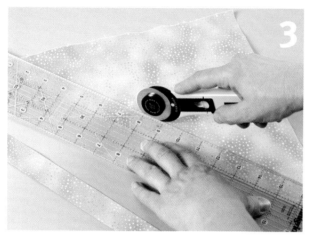

1. Working on the true bias of the stem fabric, position the edge of ruler the desired strip width from the fabric's cut edge. Cut bias strips three times the desired final width. For example, for a 3/8"-wide finished stem cut 1-1/8"-wide strips.

2. With wrong sides together, press slightly more than one-third of the strip width up.

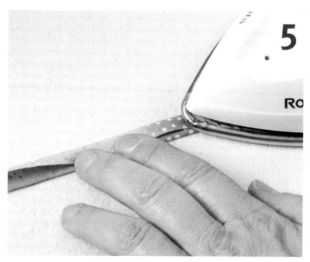

3. Fold the remaining fabric over the first edge, folding the strip in thirds. Press.

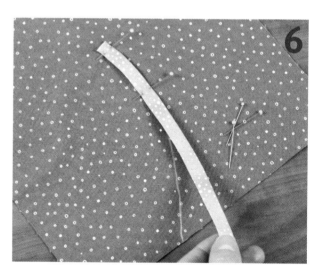

4. Cut to desired stem lengths plus a few extra inches. Mark the stem position on the appliqué background. Position the folded stem in place straddling the marked line and curving as desired. Pin or baste in place.

Appliqué Inspirations

FLOWERING TRELLIS

Lesson nine

Putting It All Together

What you need to know about putting it all together

Now that you have mastered the individual lessons, it is time to use the techniques on a small project.

valentine flower

finished size: 10-1/2"

Follow these step-by-step photo directions to make this colorful heart-petaled quilt.

Materials

Fabric suggestions are 40"-42" wide. Sew all patchwork seams with a 1/4" seam allowance. Follow manufacturer's temperature directions for using paper-backed fusible web.
Fat quarter = 18" x 20"

- 1 fat quarter off-white print for background
- 1 fat quarter green print for borders and leaf appliqué
- 1 fat quarter hot pink for corner posts and flower appliqué
- 1 fat quarter coordinating green print for backing and binding
- Scraps of yellow and orange prints for appliqué
- 1/4 yard paper-backed fusible web
- 14" x 14" piece of quilt batting

Select Appliqué and Fabrics

1. In this lesson we will work through the steps from previous lessons using the motifs on page 102.

2. One of the easiest ways to select fabric is to find a print you like and take your color cues from it. Be sure to select a variety of values as well as colors. Here I used the multi colored print for the binding and backing.

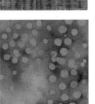

NOTE: *Make a few extra appliqué motifs to practice your stitching. It is also a good idea to save a few of the trimmings to make stitch samples as discussed in Lesson 7.*

Cut the Fabrics

From the off-white print, cut:

- 1—9" square for background

From the green print, cut:

- 4—1-1/2" x 8-1/2" rectangles for borders

From the hot pink print, cut:

- 4—1-1/2" squares for corner posts

From the coordinating green print, cut:

- 1—10" square for backing
- 3—2-1/4"-wide strips for binding

Prepare the Appliqué

1. Referring to Lessons 3 and 4, select the type of appliqué preparation you wish to use. In the example, we are using the fused appliqué technique in Lesson 3. The patterns for the appliqué are found on page 102 and the Valentine Flower layout diagram is found on page 103.
   Make the following appliqué pieces referring to the photo on page 76 for color choices:

Flower

   4—Petal A
   2—Petal B
   1—Leaf
   1—Center A
   1—Center B

2. Trace the appliqué patterns onto the fusible web. Mark the pattern name and fuse to selected fabrics. Cut out the appliqué pieces.

3. Using the green print fabric and referring to Lesson 8, prepare 6" of 1/4"-wide bias stem.

4. Make a copy of the Valentine Flower Layout on page 103. Lay a nonstick pressing sheet over the layout. Fuse the flower motifs together on the nonstick pressing sheet. Refer to Lesson 5 for more information.

5. Find the center of the background fabric by folding it in quarters referring to photo 4 on page 41. Position the layout under the background matching the centers. Use the layout as a guide to position the stem, flower, and leaf.

Select and Practice Stitching

1. Select the stitches you would like to use. Fuse the extra motifs and trimmings to a leftover piece of background fabric.

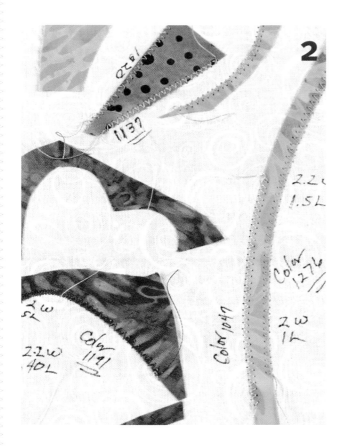

2. Practice stitching until you find the width and length you want to use. Next, try a few different thread colors to see which looks best with the motifs. Mark the stitch number, length, and width beside each stitch selection.

Stitch the Appliqué

1. Stitch the appliqué motifs to the background fabric beginning with the appliqué closest to the background. I used a zigzag stitch in the example. Continue stitching the appliqué pieces, working from the background up. Stitch the center circles last.

2. Trim the appliquéd center to 8-1/2" square.

Complete the Top

1. Sew 2 green print borders to opposite sides of the appliquéd center.

2. Sew 1 hot pink print corner post to each end of the remaining green print borders. Sew borders to top and bottom of the appliquéd center.

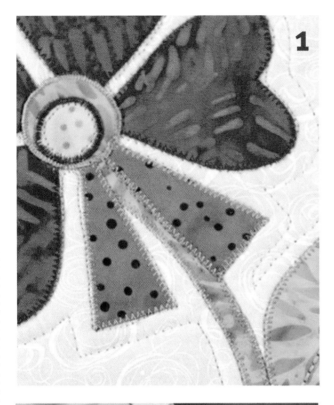

Finishing the Quilt

1. Layer quilt top with backing and batting. Stitch in the ditch of the border seams. Free-motion quilt around the motifs using invisible thread or thread to match the background. Quilt the background as desired.

2. Sew the 2-1/4"-wide binding strips together with diagonal seams to make a continuous strip. Use to bind the quilt.

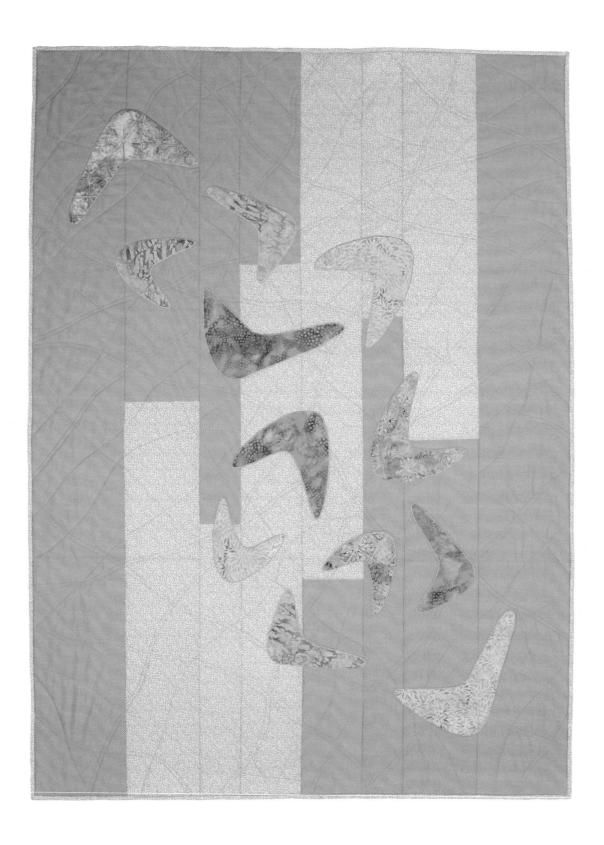

boomerang lap throw

finished size: 40" x 55"

The combination of gray and turquoise colors and a boomerang-shaped motif create a retro-looking throw that is quick to stitch together.

Materials

Fabric suggestions are 40"-42" wide. Sew all patchwork seams with a 1/4" seam allowance. Follow manufacturer's directions for using paper-backed fusible web.
Fat quarter = 18" x 20".

- 1-1/2 yards gray solid fabric for background strips

- 1-1/2 yards light gray print fabric for background strips and binding

- 2 fat quarters blue/turquoise print fabric for appliqué

- 2 fat quarters green/chartreuse print fabric for appliqué

- 1-3/4 yards backing fabric
  Note: If a longarm machine is to be used for quilting, you will need 2-3/4 yards for a pieced back.

- 1-1/4 yards paper-backed fusible web

- 46" x 61" piece quilt batting or crib-size batting

Cut the Fabrics

From the gray solid, cut:
- 2—7-1/2" x 39-1/2" A rectangles
- 2—7-1/2" x 16-1/2" B rectangles
- 2—6" x 26-1/2" C rectangles
- 2—3-1/2" x 35-1/2" E rectangles
- 2—5" x 16-1/2" G rectangles

From the light gray print, cut:
- 2—6" x 29-1/2" D rectangles
- 2—3-1/2" x 20-1/2" F rectangles
- 2—5" x 39-1/2" H rectangles
- 6—2-1/4"-wide strips for binding

Prepare the Appliqué

Referring to Lessons 3 and 4, select the type of appliqué preparation you wish to use. In the example, we are using the fused appliqué technique in Lesson 3. The patterns for the appliqué are found on pages 104-105.

Trace and prepare the following boomerangs referring to the quilt photo on page 84 for color choices:

Boomerangs
    3—Boomerang A
    3—Boomerang B
    3—Boomerang C
    3—Boomerang D

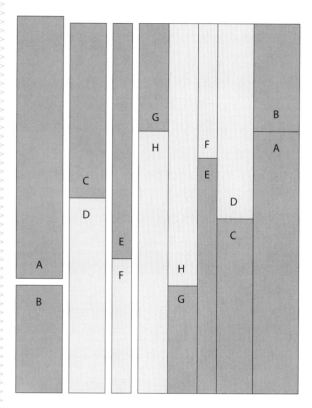

Assemble the Quilt

1. The quilt center is made in vertical columns. Sew together one rectangle A and one rectangle B along the short edges. Repeat with the remaining A and B rectangles. Join the C and D, E and F, and G and H rectangles in the same manner, making two sets of each.

2. Referring to the diagram, sew the sets together to make quilt top.

Stitch the Appliqué

1. Referring to the illustrations and photo, arrange the boomerangs on the pieced quilt top. Fuse or pin in place.

2. Following the instructions in Lessons 6 and 7, stitch the appliqué shapes in place with a satin zigzag stitch using contrasting thread.

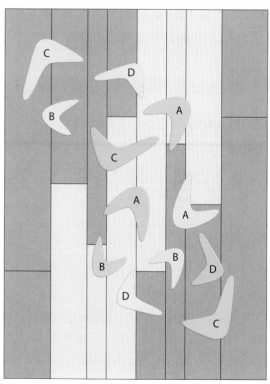

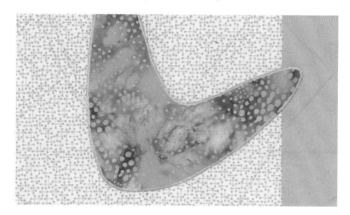

Finishing the Quilt

1. Layer the quilt top, batting, and backing.

2. Quilt around each boomerang and quilt the background as desired.

4. Trim the excess batting and backing to straighten the edges and square the corners.

5. Stitch the 2-1/4"-wide light gray strips together with diagonal seams to make one continuous strip. Use the strip to bind the quilt.

Appliqué Inspirations

IRRESISTIBLE IRIS

flower accent pillow

finished size: 16" x 12"

Pillows are a great way to introduce accent colors into your decor. The flower appliqués can be made in colors similar to the ones shown or in your favorite hues.

Materials

Fabric suggestions are 40"-42" wide. Sew all patchwork seams with a 1/4" seam allowance. Follow manufacturer's directions for using paper-backed fusible web.

Fat quarter = 18" x 20".

- 1-1/4 yards light gray solid for pillow background, lining, and back

- 5 - 6 assorted print fat quarters in aqua, red, purple, and peach for appliqué

- 1 yard paper-backed fusible web

- 18" x 14" piece quilt batting

- 16" x 12" pillow form

Cut the Fabrics

From light gray solid, cut:

- 1—18" x 14" rectangle for pillow background
- 1—19" x 15" rectangle for pillow lining
- 2—19" x 13" rectangles for pillow back

Prepare the Appliqué

1. Referring to Lessons 3 and 4, select the type of appliqué preparation you wish to use. In the example, we are using the fused appliqué technique in Lesson 3. The patterns and layouts for the appliqués are found on pages 106-107.

Trace and prepare the following appliqué pieces referring to the photo on page 88 for color choices:

Flower 1
1—Circle A
1—Circle C
1—Circle E
1—Wavy A

Flower 2
3—Circle D
3—Circle E
3—Wavy B

Flower 3
5—Circle B
5—Circle D
5—Circle E

2. Fuse the motifs together on a nonstick pressing sheet.

Arrange the Appliqué

1. Arrange the flower motifs on the background rectangle, referring to the diagram. Begin with the flowers closest to the background and work up.

2. Fuse in place.

Stitch the Appliqué

1. Following the instructions in Lessons 6 and 7, stitch the flowers to the background rectangle using stitches from Lesson 7 or other programmed stitches as suggested in the decorative stitching section on pages 64-67.

2. For added impact use contrasting thread for some of the stitching.

Assemble the Pillow Top

1. Layer the appliquéd background rectangle, batting, and lining.

2. Quilt as desired. Pillow shown has quilting just inside the flower edge and around many of the flower parts. Since the flowers are so close together it is not necessary to quilt the background.

3. Trim the quilted pillow top to 17" x 13".

Finish the Pillow

1. Fold each back rectangle in half with wrong sides facing, making two 9-1/2" x 13" rectangles.

2. Lay the back rectangles together overlapping the folded edges to make a 17" x 13" rectangle.

3. Baste across the overlap to hold in place while joining to pillow top.

4. With right sides together, lay the pillow top on the pillow back.

5. Sew around all four sides with a 1/4" seam allowance. Trim the corners.

6. Turn the pillow right side out. Lightly press the outside edge and corners.

7. Insert pillow form.

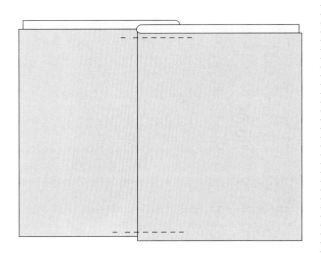

butterfly tote

finished size: 15" x 11"

The two pockets on the outside of this tote make it easy to find your cell phone or keys.

Materials

Fabric suggestions are 40"-42" wide. Sew all patchwork seams with a 1/4" seam allowance. Follow manufacturer's directions for using paper-backed fusible web.
Fat quarter = 18" x 20".

- 3/4 yard light aqua print for tote front and back
- 1 yard blue/green print for tote lining and trim
- 1 fat quarter royal blue print for tote pockets and appliqué
- 1 fat quarter dark blue dotted print for tote pockets and appliqué
- 1 fat quarter aqua print for tote pockets and appliqué
- 1 fat quarter fuchsia print for appliqué
- 1/4 yard paper-backed fusible web
- 10" x 20" piece quilt batting for pockets
- 14" x 18" piece quilt batting for tote front
- 18" x 18" piece quilt batting for tote back
- 1 pair purchased handles with 3/4" wide ring attachments

Cut the Fabrics

From the light aqua print, cut:
- 2—15-1/2" x 11-1/2" rectangles for tote front background and tote back
- 1—2-1/2" x 30-1/2" rectangle for facing
- 1—9-1/2" x 4-1/2" rectangle for tote bottom
- 1—16" x 3" rectangle for tabs

Note: If the handle connecting rings are larger than 3/4", add an extra 1" to the 3" measure of the tab rectangle for every 1/4" extra width.

From the blue/green print, cut:
- 1—20" x 11" rectangle for pocket lining
- 1—18" x 14" rectangle for front lining
- 1—18" square for back lining

From the royal blue print fat quarter, cut:
- 1—1-3/4" x 20" rectangle for pocket

From the dark blue dotted print fat quarter, cut:
- 1—2-1/4" x 20" rectangle for pocket
- 1—4" x 20" rectangle for pocket

From the aqua print fat quarter, cut:
- 1—2-1/2" x 20" rectangle for pocket

Prepare and Arrange the Appliqué Pieces

1. Referring to Lessons 3 and 4, select the type of appliqué preparation you wish to use. In the example, we are using the fused appliqué technique in Lesson 3. If you prefer to use the turned-edge technique in Lesson 4, use the alternate pattern with circle designs instead of arcs on the butterfly wings. The patterns and layout diagram for the butterfly appliqué are found on page 112.

Referring to the photo on page 92 for color choices, trace and prepare the following appliqué pieces using the remaining fabrics from the fat quarters:

Butterfly

 1—Wing A
 1—Wing B
 1—Wing C
 1—Wing D
 1—Arc A
 1—Arc B
 1—Arc C
 1—Arc D
 1—Arc E
 1—Arc F
 1—Body

2. Fuse the butterfly motif together on a nonstick pressing sheet.

3. Referring to the diagram, position the butterfly on the tote front background rectangle approximately 1" from the top and right side.

4. Press to fuse in place.

Stitch the Appliqué

1. Stitch the butterfly using a narrow satin zigzag stitch. Refer to Lesson 7, page 56.

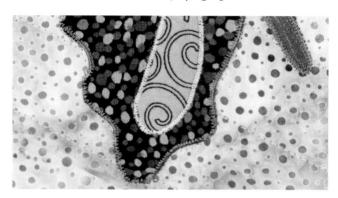

2. For extra impact use contrasting thread for some of the stitching.

Assemble the Pocket Section

1. Sew the 4—20"-long rectangles together along a long edge to make a strip set.

2. With right sides together, sew the strip set and pocket lining rectangle together along the top edge. Press the seam toward the pocket lining.

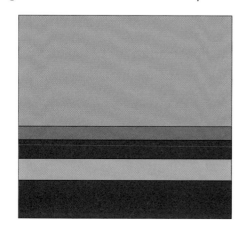

3. Fold the pocket lining rectangle to the wrong side leaving a seam allowance width of trim on the right side.

4. Insert a 10" x 20" piece of batting between the strip set and the lining. Quilt the pocket section by stitching in the ditch of all the seams.

Assemble the Front and Back

1. Matching centers, stitch the tote bottom rectangle to the tote back rectangle.

2. Layer pieced back/bottom, batting, and back lining. Quilt with parallel diagonal lines.

3. Trim batting and backing to the same size as the tote back.

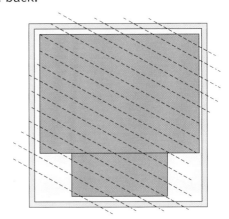

4. Layer tote front, batting, and front lining. Quilt by stitching around the butterfly and with diagonal lines on the background. Trim batting and backing to the same size as the tote front.

5. Trim both the front and back to make them narrower at the bottom by cutting a wedge off each side. Start 1" in from the side on

the bottom edge and taper to a point at the top corner.

6. Position the quilted pocket section on the tote front 3" down from the top on the left side and 1" up from the bottom on the right side. Trim to match shape of tote front. Baste pocket section in place along the edges.

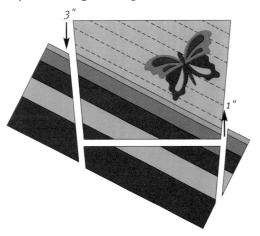

7. To form the pockets, make a double line of stitching on the pocket section about 3-3/4" in from the left side and another double line of stitching 3-1/2" to the right of that line. Stitching should be perpendicular to the bottom.

Assemble the Tote

1. Matching the centers, stitch the tote bottom rectangle to the front bottom edge. Zigzag stitch or serge the raw edges of the seams.

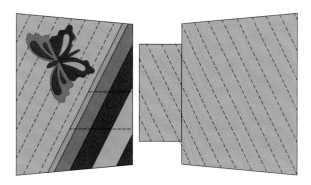

2. Layer the tote's front and back pieces together, right sides facing. Stitch the front to the back at the side seams. Zigzag stitch or serge the raw edges of the seams.

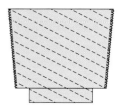

3. Fold one bottom corner opening in, aligning the side seam with the center of the bottom edge. Stitch to form bottom corner. Stitch again to reinforce the seam. Zigzag stitch or serge the edges. Repeat on the other side.

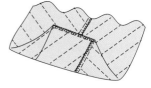

4. Join the ends of the facing rectangle to form a continuous strip. Press 1/2" of one of the strip's long edges to the wrong side.

5. With right sides together, stitch the other edge of facing to the top of the bag.

6. Press seam toward facing. Under-stitch facing and seam allowance together about 1/8" from the seam.

7. Press facing to the inside of tote. Hand-stitch the facing to the lining, taking tucks at the side seams to fit the taper of the side.

Finishing the Tote

1. Press the tab rectangle in half lengthwise, wrong sides together, to create a center fold. Open and press both edges so they meet at the center fold. Repress tab in half; concealing raw edges. Topstitch approximately 1/8" from both edges.

2. Cut the tab strip into 4—4" lengths.

3. Determine the position of the handles on the front and back of the tote by centering them and marking connection points with a pin at the top of the opening.

4. Place a tab section through the handle ring. Fold tab in half over ring. Fold raw ends of tab to wrong side about 3/4" from the cut edges.

5. To secure handle to one side, topstitch both tabs to the tote positioning them so the handle connection is about 1/2" above the top edge of the tote. Stitch a square and then an "X" as shown. Repeat on the other side.

tip:

Quick Appliqué Projects

Frequently an appliqué motif can be added to purchased items to give them added pizzazz or make them coordinate with other appliquéd items.

1. For a coordinating pillow to the Flower Accent Pillow project, I chose to appliqué Flower 1 on page 106 to the center of a 22" purchased pillow. Be sure the purchased pillow has a zipper that goes the length of one side. Remove the pillow insert and stitch on the motif. If the pillow cover is too bulky, remove the table from your sewing machine and use the free arm.

2. Liven up a kitchen or bath with appliquéd towels. I chose Flower 2 on page 107 in colors that coordinate with the kitchen towels I purchased. Satin zigzag and other decorative stitches enliven the appliqué.

3. Stitch an appliqué motif to a pocket and add the pocket to a purchased tote or purse to change it from plain to spectacular. Because stitching a motif to a tote or bag by machine would be difficult, make a lined pocket that can be added to the tote. Determine the size pocket you want, including seam allowances, and cut 2 pieces to that size. Stitch the motif, I chose the Daisy on page 109, to one piece, back it with thin batting and quilt. Place the pieces right sides together and stitch leaving approximately 4" open for turning. Turn right side out and stitch the opening closed. Pin the pocket to the tote and stitch the sides and bottom. If the bag is too bulky, remove the table from your sewing machine and use the free arm.

winter rose table runner

finished size: 36" x 18"

Make this table runner in four colorways to add seasonal decor to your table top.

Materials

Fabric suggestions are 40"-42" wide. Sew all patchwork seams with a 1/4" seam allowance. Follow manufacturer's directions for using paper-backed fusible web.
Fat quarter = 18" x 20".

- 1/3 yard white print fabric for background
- 1/3 yard lavender dotted print fabric for background
- 1/2 yard red/lavender print fabric for borders
- 1/3 yard lavender print fabric for binding
- 1 fat-quarter red print fabric for rose appliqués
- 1/2 yard green print fabric for stem and leaf appliqués
- Scraps of peach print fabric for flower center appliqués
- 2/3 yard backing fabric
- 1 yard paper-backed fusible web
- 24" x 44" piece quilt batting

Cut the Fabrics

From the white print, cut:
- 2—8" x 17" rectangles

From the lavender dotted print, cut:
- 2—8" x 17" rectangles

From the red/lavender print, cut:
- 2—2-1/2" x 36-1/2" rectangles
- 2—2-1/2" x 14-1/2" rectangles

From the lavender print, cut:
- 3—2-1/4" strips for binding

Prepare the Appliqué

Referring to Lessons 3 and 4, select the type of appliqué preparation you wish to use. In the example, we are using the fused appliqué technique in Lesson 3. The patterns and layouts for the appliqués are found on pages 110-111.

Trace and prepare the following appliqué pieces referring to the photo on page 98 for color choices:

Winter Rose
2—Petal A
2—Petal B
2—Petal C
2—Petal D
2—Petal E
2—Center

Bias Stems

Note: Cut the bias stems before fusing the leaf patterns to the fabric.

- 2—23" strips of 3/8"-wide bias stems

Leaves

    6—Leaf A

    4—Leaf B

    2—Leaf C

Assemble the Background

1. Arrange the white print and lavender dotted print rectangles as shown. Join into rows.

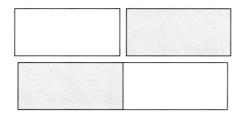

2. Sew rows together to complete the table runner background.

Arrange and Stitch the Appliqué

1. Fuse each winter rose motif together on a nonstick pressing sheet.

2. Arrange the bias stems, winter roses and leaves on the background. Fuse or pin in place.

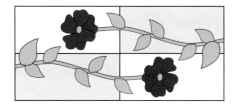

3. Following the instructions in Lessons 6 and 7, stitch the appliqué shapes in place using matching and contrasting thread. Enhance the flower centers and leaf edges using programmed stitches as suggested in the decorative stitching section on pages 64-67.

Assemble the Table Runner

1. Trim the appliquéd background to 32-1/2" x 14-1/2", centering the middle seam.

2. Sew the 2-1/2" x 14-1/2" borders to opposite ends of the appliquéd center.

3. Sew the 2-1/2" x 36-1/2" borders to the top and bottom of the appliquéd center as shown.

Finish the Table Runner

1. Layer the table runner top, batting and backing.

2. Quilt around each motif and stem using invisible thread. Quilt the background and borders as desired.

3. Trim the excess batting, and backing to straighten the edges and square the corners.

4. Stitch the 2-1/4"-wide binding strips together with diagonal seams to make one continuous strip. Use to bind the quilt.

tip:

For other seasonal table runners select your choice from the ideas below. For Summer Cone Flower and Autumn Chrysanthemum use the Daisy patterns on page 108.

Springtime Wild Rose

Summer Cone Flower

Autumn Chrysanthemum

Valentine Flower Patterns

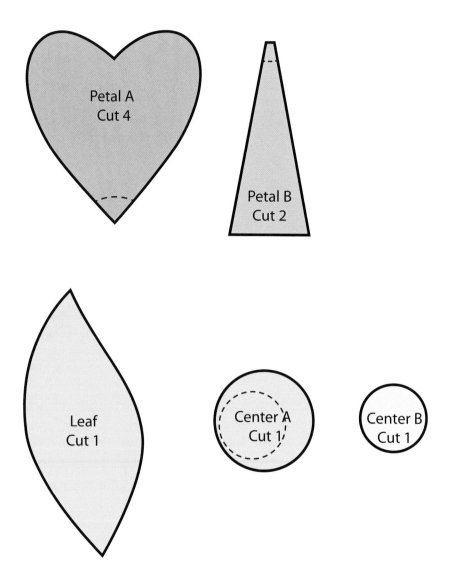

Valentine Flower Layout

+ = center of layout

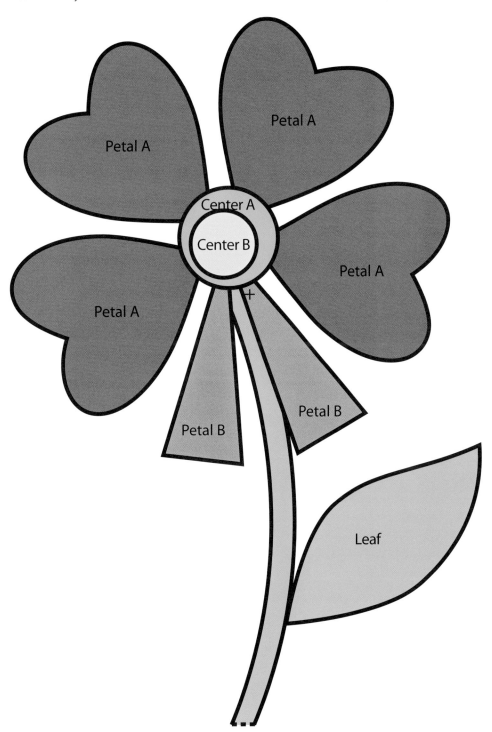

Boomerang Lap Throw Patterns

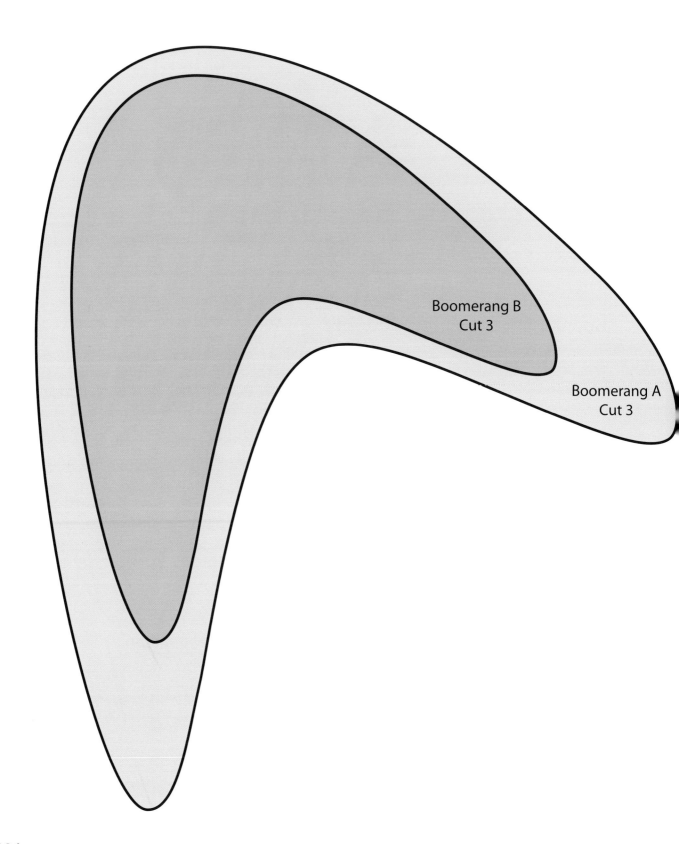

Boomerang B
Cut 3

Boomerang A
Cut 3

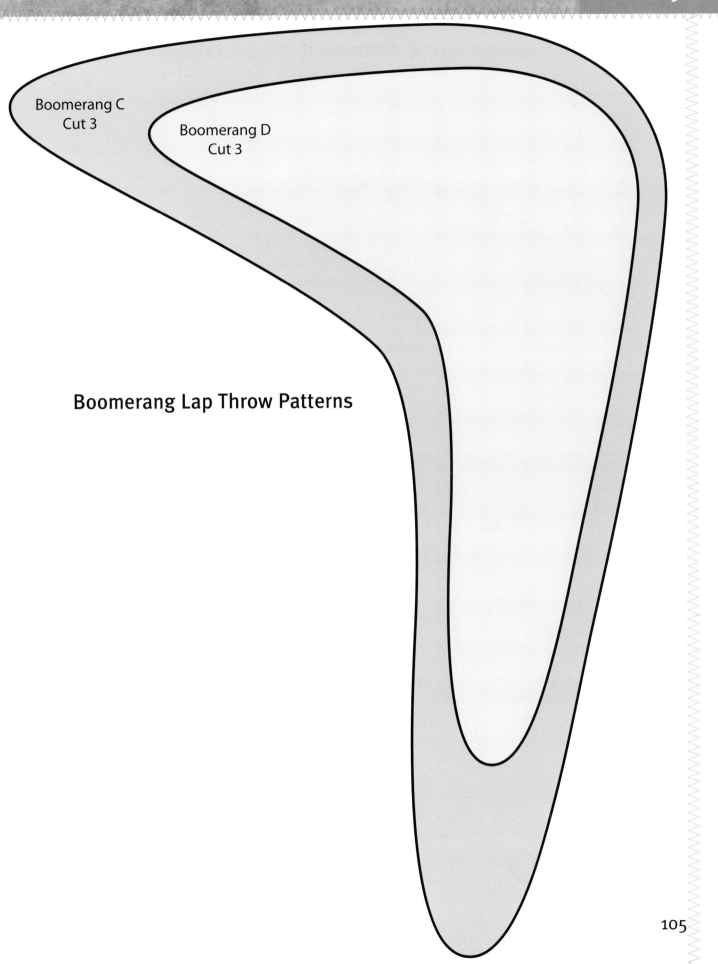

Boomerang C
Cut 3

Boomerang D
Cut 3

Boomerang Lap Throw Patterns

Flower Accent Pillow Patterns and Layout

Flower 1

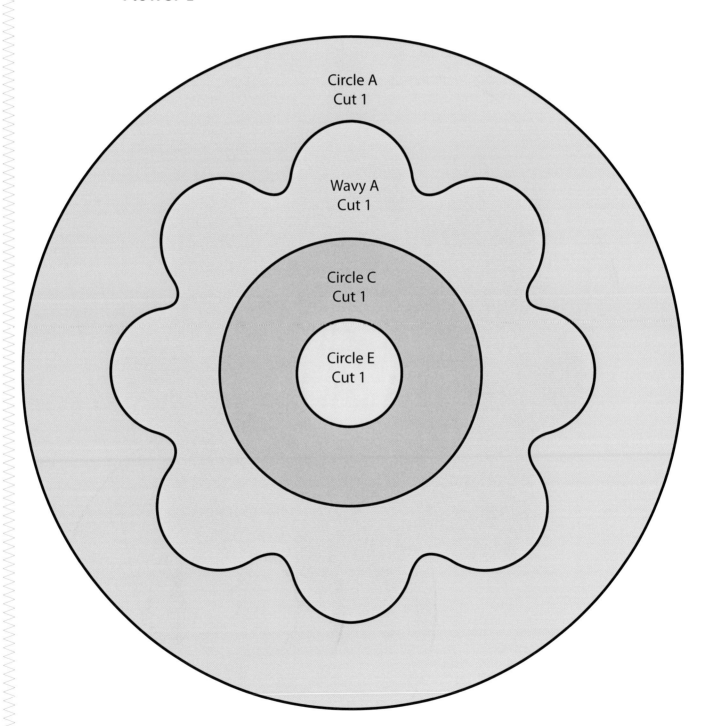

Flower Accent Pillow Patterns and Layout

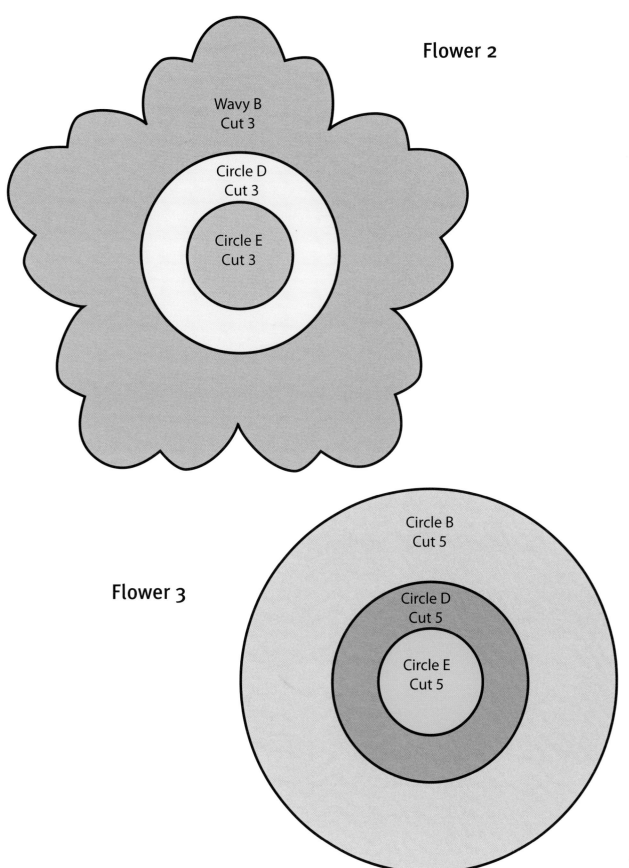

Flower 2

Wavy B
Cut 3

Circle D
Cut 3

Circle E
Cut 3

Flower 3

Circle B
Cut 5

Circle D
Cut 5

Circle E
Cut 5

Daisy Patterns

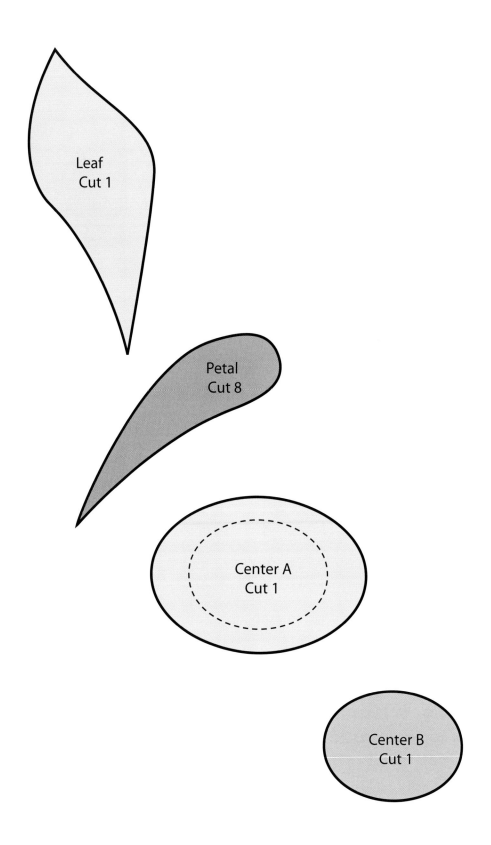

Leaf
Cut 1

Petal
Cut 8

Center A
Cut 1

Center B
Cut 1

Daisy Layout

+ = center of layout

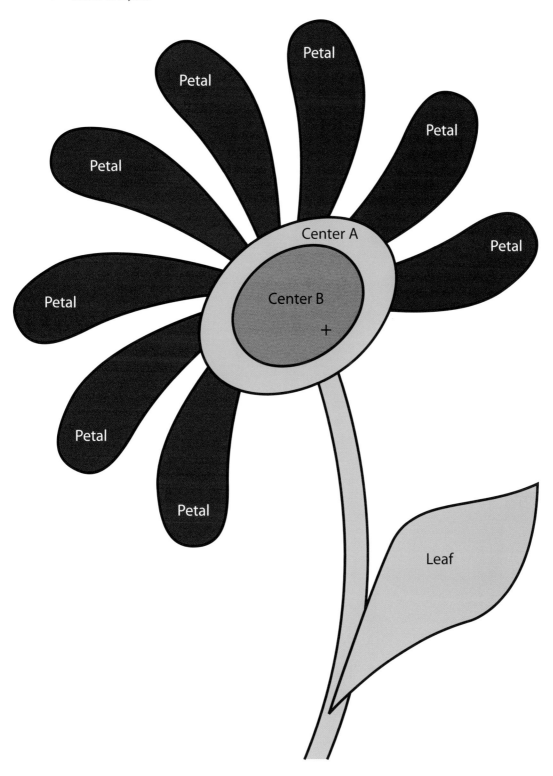

Winter Rose Patterns

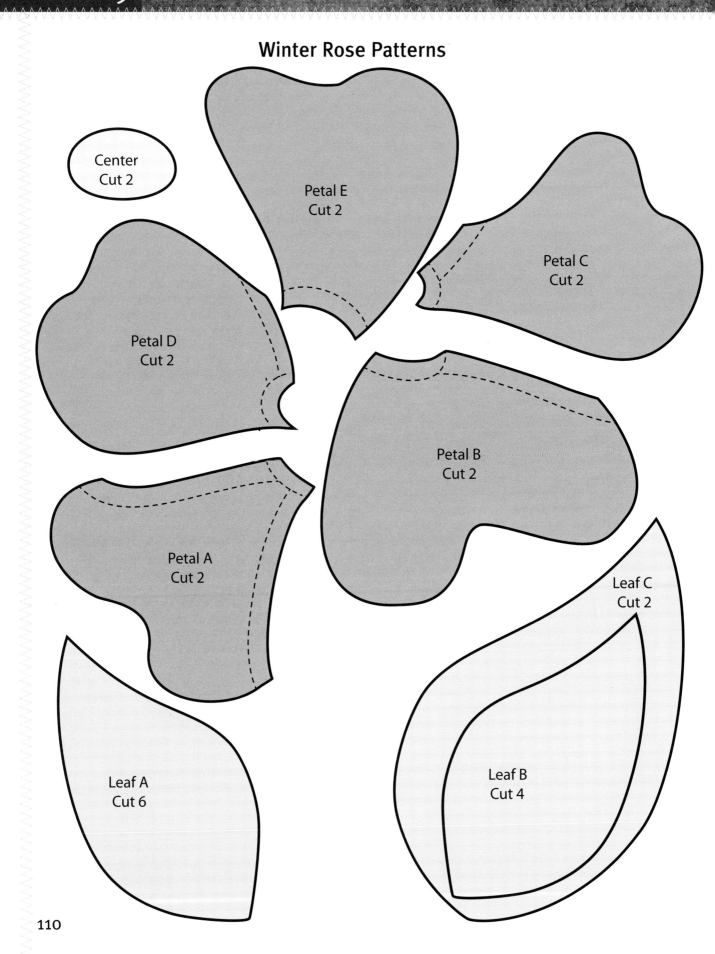

Center
Cut 2

Petal E
Cut 2

Petal C
Cut 2

Petal D
Cut 2

Petal B
Cut 2

Petal A
Cut 2

Leaf C
Cut 2

Leaf A
Cut 6

Leaf B
Cut 4

Winter Rose Layout

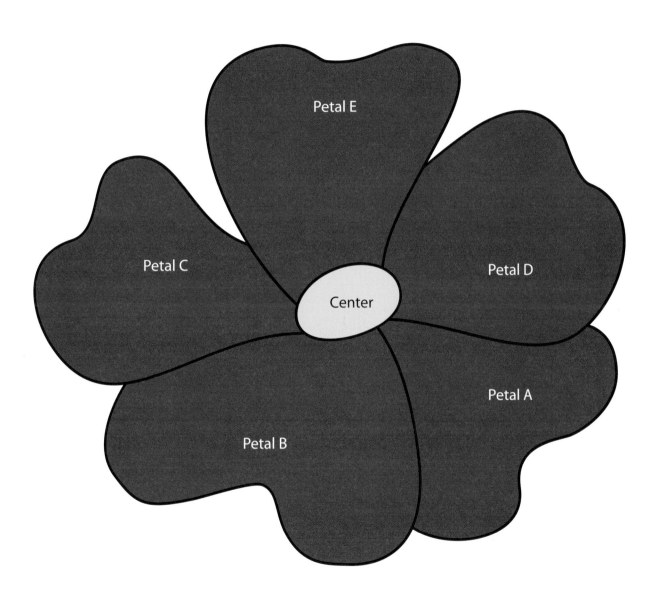

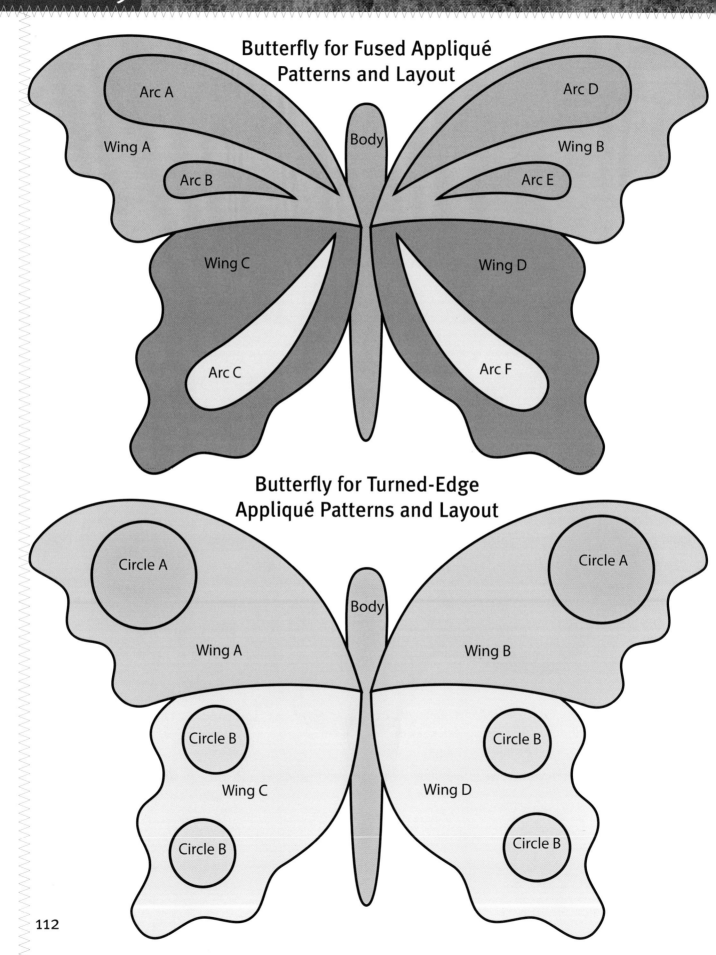

Butterfly for Fused Appliqué Patterns and Layout

Arc A

Wing A

Arc B

Body

Arc D

Wing B

Arc E

Wing C

Wing D

Arc C

Arc F

Butterfly for Turned-Edge Appliqué Patterns and Layout

Circle A

Circle A

Body

Wing A

Wing B

Circle B

Circle B

Wing C

Wing D

Circle B

Circle B